Managing Computer Projects

BCS Practitioner Series

Series editor: Ray Welland

Managing Computer Projects

Avoiding the pitfalls

Robin Gibson

Prentice Hall

New York London Toronto Sydney Tokyo Singapore

First published 1992 by
Prentice Hall International (UK) Ltd
Campus 400, Maylands Avenue
Hemel Hempstead
Hertfordshire, HP2 7EZ
A division of
Simon & Schuster International Group

Typeset in 10/12 pt Times
by MHL Typesetting Ltd., Coventry

Printed and bound in Great Britain by
Dotesios Limited, Trowbridge, Wiltshire

Library of Congress Cataloging-in-Publication Data

Gibson, Robin, 1927–
    Managing computer projects: avoiding the pitfalls / Robin
Gibson.
        p. cm. -- (BCS practitioner series)
    Includes bibliographical references and index.
    ISBN 0-13-159591-1 (pbk.)
    1. Systems design. 2. Computer software--Development. I. Title.
II. Series.
QA76.9.S88G44   1992
004.2'1--dc20   92-7781
                                                                   CIP

---

1 2 3 4 5 96 95 94 93 92

A catalogue record for this book is available from the British Library

ISBN 0-13-159591-1

Contents

Editorial preface

The aim of the BCS Practitioner Series is to produce books which are relevant for practising computer professionals across the whole spectrum of Information Technology activities. We want to encourage practitioners to share their practical experience of methods and applications with fellow professionals. We also seek to disseminate information in a form which is suitable for the practitioner who often has only limited time to read widely within a new subject area or to assimilate research findings.

The role of the BCS is to provide advice on the suitability of books for the Series, via the Editorial Panel, and to provide a pool of potential authors upon which we can draw. Our objective is that this Series will reinforce the drive within the BCS to increase professional standards in IT. The other partners in this venture, Prentice Hall, provide the publishing expertise and international marketing capabilities of a leading publisher in the computing field.

The response when we set up the Series was extremely encouraging. However, the success of the Series depends on there being practitioners who want to learn as well as those who feel they have something to offer! The Series is under continual development and we are always looking for ideas for new topics and feedback on how to further improve the usefulness of the Series. If you are interested in writing for the Series then please contact us.

Cost estimation for software projects is a problem area with many well-publicised disasters. This book offers practical advice about realistic cost estimation based on the author's extensive experience in the field. The emphasis of this book is on the practice of cost estimation, not the theory, and useful summaries of techniques are included as appendices.

Ray Welland
Computing Science Department, University of Glasgow

Editorial Panel Members
Frank Bott (UCW, Aberystwyth), John Harrison (BAe Sema), Nic Holt (ICL), Trevor King (Praxis Systems Plc), Tom Lake (GLOSSA), Kathy Spurr (Analysis and Design Consultants), Mario Wolczko (University of Manchester)

Foreword

As President of the British Computer Society, I am pleased to be able to launch this book in the new 'Practitioner' series, sponsored by the BCS, which aims to help those engaged in the practical application of computers. The present book will be followed by others so that the lessons of the most experienced people may be passed on.

I have a particular interest in the subject of this book, since I have been involved with all aspects of computer projects, ranging from supervising programming teams in the late 1950s and early 1960s through to the authorisation of some of the largest pioneering projects in more recent times. Many of these have also closely involved the author of this book.

My interest also stems from the fact that I continue to read banner headlines in the technical press announcing yet another major project delay, massive cost over-run or, indeed, cancellation. The old excuse that the industry is still in its formative stage will no longer wash. Examples of successes are still all too rare. Why is this, when many of the management and control techniques must have been understood by the Chinese when they built the Great Wall or by the Egyptians when they built the Pyramids?

One becomes accustomed to the seemingly inevitable problems and headaches of these projects, particularly when they have been contracted out on a fixed-cost basis, but one of the lessons I learned is the importance of good rapport, a close relationship, and mutual respect among the principal personnel involved — the purchaser, the user and the project manager. The key person who has most influence over the course of events is the project manager. Yet it has always been very difficult to find suitable people to do this job and I hope this book helps in some way to address that problem.

I have known the author for over twenty years. He and I worked together in International Computers Limited, and latterly he became the chief trouble-shooter and supervising project manager for all the company's projects in the United Kingdom. I can therefore commend his qualifications for writing this book and if readers learn some lessons from his wide experience, it will be of considerable value.

Alan R. Rousell
President, British Computer Society
20 September 1991

Preface

This book has a crusading mission. In over thirty years of working with large bespoke computer projects, I have experienced many difficulties in trying to achieve a satisfactory result, on time and to budget. Having now reflected on the issues, some solutions are suggested to overcome the difficulties — or at least to reduce their impact.

The subject is limited to the productive aspects of the task — the development of a system which meets the stated requirement — and it does not address how computers should be applied in a particular business.

In recent years, purchasers have attempted to solve the problem by imposing fixed-price terms on contractors. However, this approach does not guarantee a successful outcome — just as selecting the lowest bid by a builder does not mean that the constructional project will be satisfactory — and a computer project has some special hazards.

What are these?

Firstly, computer projects are not like constructional projects. The amount of routine, predictable work is relatively small and much is of an intellectual nature. Furthermore, the detailed design of the system is not complete until about half-way through the project; yet commitment to the project is usually made earlier, when the design is only in outline and when it is difficult to make reliable projections of the cost and timescale.

Secondly, although there has been steady improvement in the technical aspects of the development process, techniques are still changing and there is no mature standard; this applies also to management practice where the quality of the plans and of the development process are often inadequate.

Thirdly, the skills shortage in the computer industry often causes the project team to be over-stretched; qualified project managers are difficult to obtain, particularly at short notice, and many appointments are made belatedly.

These difficulties indicate some reasons why project managers often struggle — so much so that they may be overwhelmed or have an impracticable task. The history of large projects shows the desperate measures that have been taken to rescue troublesome projects — including replacement of the project manager.

Such weaknesses — unsound foundations; poor quality; inadequate skills — are not the only hazards. However, they are singled out because they are common causes of the major problems; by major, I mean those causing the cost and timescale to over-run by at least 50 per cent.

These problems can only be solved if all managers involved, including purchasers, users and senior project staff, understand the key issues and contribute to the success of the project. The book is therefore addressed to all such people. The selected challenges at the general management level are at the beginning and end of the book; those for the project manager occupy the bulk of the book, but since the technicalities have been limited, it is hoped that all the key messages will be appreciated by other involved managers, even if they have to skip over some parts.

Producing useful guidelines for managers on such wide-ranging and complex issues is not easy, especially since the difficulties have long been intractable — and there are no simple solutions. Some of the views advocated will be controversial and some of the pioneering techniques may be regarded with scepticism. Hence the book is not intended for students or junior and inexperienced staff. The reader, even if non-technical, should be sufficiently experienced to make a mature judgement about the suggestions, based on personal experience of the difficulties of practical management.

The book is therefore not a comprehensive guide for project managers, although the subjects omitted do relate mainly to the tools of the (project management) trade and the administrative mechanics of the task. Although these are important, they are either covered fully in other books or are undergoing rapid change. In any event, they are unlikely to cause the major problems and failures which this book aims to prevent.

From my experience of directing some of the largest pioneering projects, both as a line project manager and in directing several concurrent projects, I have included practical lessons learned the 'hard way' and also some new insights, developed from more recent research and consideration of other views on the international stage. I can only assert that if I had applied the suggestions in this book all my past projects would have benefited — although each project has some unique problems which cannot be covered by any book. Finally, I hope that the suggestions and views will provoke further development since there is still much to be learned.

Acknowledgements

I would like to thank some ICL colleagues, especially Mike Dolan and Mike Cave, for their constructive comments at an early stage of writing the book, and I am grateful to my former boss, Alan Rousell, for his encouragement and contribution with the foreword. I thank Dr B. Kitchenham for her most helpful advice during the development of my ideas on estimating and for her comments on a substantial part of the book. I am also grateful to the Prentice Hall team of reviewers for their detailed and helpful comments.

I am much indebted to very many past colleagues who have worked with me on a wide variety of projects over many years, and whose skills and efforts have helped me to gain the experience reflected in this book. And finally I thank my wife for her support.

Robin Gibson
December 1991

1 An outline of the challenge

1.1 Introduction

This book is concerned with controlling the development of bespoke systems for information processing. Although much of the content is relevant to all projects, there is a bias towards the larger ones — those requiring more than about twenty man-years of development effort — because these have many more problems. This chapter sets out the overall perspectives of the task, and also indicates the main themes appearing throughout the book.

Developing a new computer system is somewhat like any other constructional project which produces an end-product to meet a defined requirement. However, it is more difficult for purchasers to understand how computer systems are constructed, particularly when the technology is continuously changing. Yet those who authorise a project need to appraise the project proposal carefully, especially the pioneering aspects and major risks; and this chapter begins the process of unveiling some of the hazards.

Although projects are carried out for many different organisations, the terminology has been standardised by referring to the user of a computer system as the 'business'; the term 'purchaser' is used for the senior management who authorise a project; and the terms 'project authority', 'directing management' and 'contractor' are used for those with overall responsibility for the system development and direction of the project manager.

1.1.1 The computer system

A computer-based information system is considered as having the following three main components:

(a) a set of hardware for the input, output and storage of information; some of the units may be dispersed to form a networked system, with interconnections via communication lines;

(b) the software programs, which bring the hardware to life by processing the input data, generating the results and updating the record files;

(c) the end-users of the system who operate a keyboard to initiate the chosen processes and to obtain the required information, displayed on a screen or in printed form.

1

Since much, if not all, of the hardware is ready-made the development process is largely concerned with the production of the software, although the selection and integration of the hardware are also vital tasks.

1.2   The main challenges in developing the system

These are outlined below:

1.2.1   The design of the system

Will the design meet the stated needs and provide a cost-effective system?

A project is committed from a theoretical design of the system, rather like deciding on a film production on the basis of a written film script. However, it is much more difficult for management to appraise a system specification because it is so complex and contains much technical detail: it is also difficult to visualise the final physical system. These obstacles mean that there is a danger of placing too much trust in designers' capabilities — and not enough control by management.

Since the detailed design is not completed until more than half-way through the development timescale, it is usually necessary to authorise the project well beforehand from an intermediate design which may have some loopholes and unresolved hazards.

1.2.2   The cost and timescale

Cost and timescale estimates of a project are notoriously unreliable and are a particular problem for contractors making a fixed-price commitment. Various theoretical models have been developed to produce estimates, but their reliability is questionable — except perhaps in special environments — and any estimate depends crucially on the difficult task of forecasting the eventual size of the software.

Unfortunately, there are many different estimating practices and no standards to guide the estimator; the approach therefore depends largely on individual preferences and experience. As a result, estimates often have a weak basis and may not be endorsed by the accountable project manager since that appointment is often belated.

1.2.3   Implementing the operational system

Just two problems are highlighted as an illustration.

(i) Staffing

Even with a sound plan, a successful project depends on obtaining scarce specialists, especially a well-qualified project manager. But a project proposal may not be backed up by availability of key staff, and it may be difficult to obtain the necessary staff in time.

(ii) Software quality

Many projects are bedevilled by defects in the software programs which increase the cost and timescale and also cause unreliable operation. Avoiding the problem depends on meticulous processing of a vast amount of detail by the developers; but this does not happen, and there is not, as yet, a standard method for achieving good quality in software development, even though half or more of development staff time is spent on correcting defects. Despite this high cost, many defects remain when live operation begins and the teething problems delay the achievement of reliable operation.

The above problems can be eased by phasing the development and introduction of large systems. However, this is not always possible and, in any event, it is a tough challenge to transform a large bespoke development, especially one with pioneering aspects, into a rugged operational system. As an analogy, there is a big difference between developing a prototype aeroplane and producing the operational version. Yet a new computer system is expected to work reliably in a live environment as soon as it is installed — the system has to pass through the prototype stage into productive use without a period allocated for re-engineering to correct the teething problems. This is normally unavoidable because it is rarely possible to introduce new computer systems merely for testing.

1.3 The management response — a summary of the main themes of the following chapters

The above issues highlight the importance of the preparatory work prior to the business authorisation of a project. This phase includes the project planning and the appointment of the project manager, and both tasks have vital influence on the implementation. This is why the pre-commitment phase occupies much of the book.

1.3.1 Launching a project (see Chapter 2)

There is no standard form of project proposal for approval by the purchaser prior to commitment. Yet a thorough proposal is the key to a successful project. Hence, a method is described for orchestrating the preparatory work to produce a sound design and project plan, with a reliable costing and timescale forecast.

The staffing policy should ensure that a qualified project manager is appointed in good time. And, when contractors are used, the efforts of the project team need to be integrated with the purchaser's staff, who have to assist in preparing the overall system.

This chapter also provides some basic information on the author's interpretation of the project task.

1.3.2   Direction of the design (see Chapter 3)

Many managers find it difficult to direct this highly technical task, and, although much depends on the qualifications of the manager, the following minimal controls are suggested:

- deciding on the terms of reference of the task, how the design is to be formulated and assigning the roles;
- ensuring that the scope and depth of the software is adequate to provide a sound basis for implementation;
- reviewing both progress and the final design, paying special attention to the more hazardous aspects.

1.3.3   Planning and estimating (see Chapter 4)

This oft-neglected task involves scheduling and costing the activities which develop the outline design into a working system. By reviewing alternative methods, it is argued that a firm estimate needs to have a practical basis — a plan, showing how the project will be carried out, and endorsed by the potential project manager.

The suggested approach involves the following:

- forming the development strategy, including an evolutionary approach to reduce the risks;
- expressing the estimate in such a way that a risk assessment can be made by the directing management;
- separate planning of each stage of the project, and introduction of a special technique for the final tests because they are often poorly planned;
- application of 'management by exception' in assessing the project plan.

1.3.4   Detailed estimating guidelines (the Appendix)

The planning and estimating process is described in more detail in the Appendix, for the benefit of the technical practitioners. This includes details of a quantitative method for estimating the final tests.

1.3.5   Managing the project implementation (see Chapter 5)

Only the more crucial tasks are considered — especially the following:

- establishing the foundations of the project, including standards for the development process;

- achieving good quality by setting target levels for the defects which emerge during the project and by suggesting how they may be effectively controlled;
- controlling the impact of changes;
- the technical management of each development stage — up to final acceptance of the working system;
- some guidance on general management issues.

1.3.6 The project manager (see Chapter 6)

The shortage of qualified staff makes it likely that contractors will be used for the larger projects. Even big organisations find it difficult to develop in-house project skills; project managers tend to move on rapidly to other more 'attractive' fields — for example, in sales and in general management. In the military sphere, it has long been common practice, worldwide, to use specialist contractors to develop computer systems. However, where contractors are used, it is vital that the purchaser has sufficient technical expertise to direct and monitor the overall development, and because the system extends beyond the normal project boundary and must include an effective coupling with the business operation.

Selecting a project manager who is well qualified for the job is not easy, and an approach is suggested which indicates how the candidates' abilities can be gauged against the challenge of the job. The purchaser should be involved in the appointment of the project manager, even when contractors are used, since so much depends on that person's capability. All too often it is wrongly assumed that the project manager is self-sufficient — until major problems are belatedly revealed. Therefore, suggestions are offered to the directing management for improving its control of the project manager in what is usually a very challenging task.

2 The launch of a project

2.1 Introduction

In order to be confident that the implementation will meet the project objectives, management should ensure that the proposal is based not only on a sound design, but also on a practical plan for the development.

This assertion is examined and justified in this chapter as it is one of the main themes of the book.

The development of a computer system is carried out in two phases. The initial phase involves specifying the requirements and producing a project proposal which contains the system design and a plan for carrying out the second phase of the development — to implement the system. There is usually an interval between these phases when the development is interrupted until the investment decision is made to launch the project.

The main aim of the chapter is to justify a particular approach for producing the project proposal and, because this involves the purchaser as well as the project authority, the chapter is addressed to both parties. A perspective view of the total system is given in the next section, and this is followed by a basic outline of the overall development process. Then, the main hazards are summarised, with emphasis on those which cause an over-run of time-scale and cost. After reviewing the resourcing issues and how contractors may be used, it is shown how the production and content of a project proposal need to be carefully orchestrated — this is the way to ensure that the project will be built on sound foundations.

2.2 The 'total system'

The computer system considered in this book is assumed to include a new set of hardware as well as bespoke software — and it also includes the users. Therefore, three elements are involved in creating the system: the hardware; the software; and preparations for using the system. All three elements interact closely in the development — and this is why the concept of the 'total system' is so important.

However, the project task does not cover the total system. It includes the major development for the software and the provision of the hardware, but it may not provide other physical resources, such as a communication network and the accommodation and environmental facilities; and it may not cover the preparations for using the system. Furthermore, the project does not cover the operation and maintenance of the system; it has a limited timescale — until the system has been built and accepted.

The purchaser and users are also somewhat blinkered. They can appreciate and understand how to communicate with the computer system — the man-machine interface — and this may be emphasised when ordering a system. But they may not appreciate how the system is limited by its technical design; for example, sometimes too much is expected of the system performance — and there is not enough awareness that the system cannot be loaded beyond its limits without slowing its response. Purchasers and users must therefore be responsible for prescribing the system limits, and should understand that these cannot easily be changed.

Although the need for close collaboration between the development team and the users is self-evident, it often does not happen — users cannot be expected to understand the technical complexities. Pragmatically, the best solution is for the developers to take the initiative in helping the users. Unfortunately, commercial pressures often restrict such flexibility, and developers are blinkered because they are preoccupied with their own committed work — especially in developing the bespoke software. And, for a large system, this is such a tough and challenging task, that the project team is often under great pressure, in struggling with technical problems, to avoid delays and cost over-runs. Reducing these pressures depends on laying sound foundations for the development; and it is the joint effort of both parties in this task which provides the basis for developing the total system.

2.3   An outline of the development process

The staffing profile of a project is shown in Figure 2.1, and this indicates the relatively long duration and low staffing level of the initial phase. The development process usually begins with a feasibility study to identify the main requirements, and to assess if these may be met by a practical and affordable system. If there is a positive conclusion, a detailed analysis is then carried out to define the 'system requirements' which form the basis for the creative design work. The system design provides the blueprint for producing all components of the system; this allows the software programs to be produced, and they are then integrated and combined with the hardware so that the complete system can be tested prior to its introduction for operational use. However, in parallel with the development of the computer system, preparations also have to be made for the operation, use and maintenance of the system.

In practice, there is a discontinuity in the development process, after the design phase, to allow time for the business decision as to whether to proceed with the project. The decision is based on a project proposal which contains the design architecture, plus the costed plans for the implementation and operation of the system. The nature of the proposal is indicated in Figure 2.2. This shows that the design architecture may be regarded as having two main 'products': a

Figure 2.1
Development staffing
profile

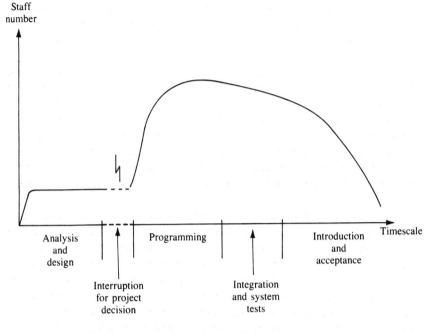

Figure 2.2 The
composition of the
project proposal

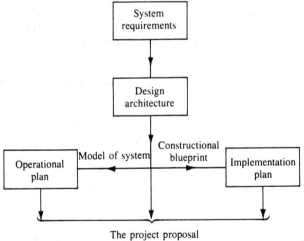

constructional blueprint, which is the basis for the remaining development; and a theoretical model or specification to show how the requirements are met for the operational system. If the proposal is accepted, the development activity moves on to the project phase where the nature of the development changes, from being an exploratory study to being a well-defined task.

2.3.1   *The sequence of activities*

(i) The initial phase — analysis and design

The requirement specification should describe all of the data to flow into and out of the system and how it is to be processed and validated. This involves analysing the information needs of the business, using staff with knowledge of how the system will be used; in contrast, the design of the computer system is a specialised technical task which is not completed at a detailed level until about half-way through the project timescale. Consequently, the decision to authorise the project has to be made when the design is only at some intermediate level, which is referred to as the 'Architectural Design'.

The design is not only based on the information needs; it is also affected by the operational requirements which specify how well the system should perform, for example its speed of response, its ease of use and its reliability. But, whilst the requirements should not be influenced too strongly by design considerations, the system has to be practicable and affordable. This involves some interaction between the requirements and the design; then some requirements can be modified or relaxed as a trade-off to improve the cost-effectiveness of the system.

The design of a large system is usually divided up into sub-systems to make the development task more manageable; the work can then be phased into successive increments so that the initial sub-system becomes operational at a relatively early date. Although such an approach may increase the overall timescale, it avoids the dangers of a 'big bang' implementation. Another method for reducing risks in a pioneering development is to develop a small pilot or prototype system to test the more crucial elements.

(ii) Programming

During this stage, the design is expanded to provide a precise brief for writing the coded instructions in small modules and then testing them on a computer. Although this is the main productive stage, the work is mechanistic and predictable, so much so that it is rare for this stage to be completed late.

(iii) Integration and system testing

The coded modules are built up or 'integrated' into the loadable system, which is tested against the requirements and design specifications. These tests need to be stringent to check that the system fully meets the requirements and is fit for operational use. But the process can take several months for a large project, often with unexpected delays because most of the time is taken up in correcting software defects generated in the preceding development. And this issue is increasingly important for the larger systems because the number of defects increases with the size of the system.

(iv) Introduction and acceptance

Irrespective of whether there is an incremental form of development, the introduction of the live system is usually phased in some way. This ensures that the initial use of the system is not disrupted too much by teething problems; it also avoids over-stretching the business organisation in coping with the new system. The end of the project should then occur when the system provides a satisfactory service and meets the requirements; however, the project should also provide for a smooth transition to the 'care and maintenance' state and future development of the system.

2.4   Development hazards

Experience has shown that the outcome of most large projects falls short of expectations. Provided that the design is sufficiently sound to make the system potentially viable, the two main hazards are as follows:

1. Unsatisfactory quality of the delivered system. In a computer system, quality is gauged by the degree of compliance with the requirements, especially the occurrence of operational faults which make the system unreliable or unsatisfactory. Unfortunately, many faults only emerge after introducing the system to live work, and, even where the defects can be fully corrected, the availability of the system is delayed.
2. Excess cost and late completion of the project.

These problems may arise from the manner of conducting the project and from design and planning weaknesses, which are considered in the following chapters. However, the problems are also affected by the way in which the studies and preparations are conducted prior to launching the project and by the resourcing of the work; this applies particularly to the reliability of the cost and timescale estimates, as discussed below.

2.5   Cost and timescale estimates

One of the great unsolved problems of the computer industry is how to predict reliably the timescale and cost of a large project. Many case histories could be written of projects which failed where the cause was attributable to optimistic estimating, rather than poor project capability. In order to demonstrate how the background of the proposal affects the estimate, a possible scenario of many project proposals is described below.

Composite case history	The need for a new computer system often becomes pressing when a purchaser realises that it is feasible, and when there is a strong business case — to improve profitability or customer service or for other business reasons. These pressures often result

in a tight timescale for producing the proposal in order to expedite the launch of the project. The urgency is transmitted to those involved, and the purchaser sets a completion date for the proposal. But, even if the contractors or design managers feel that insufficient time has been allowed, the case for a longer timescale is either not made or not accepted. This commonly occurs because it is difficult, even for experienced managers, to gauge how much time is needed to produce a sound proposal; or the commercial pressures may dictate that a fixed timescale has to be met in competitive situations.

The consequence is that the scope of the proposal is often adjusted to fit the available resources and timescale. Although the system requirements may appear to be matched by the design and plans, many aspects are loosely defined and coarsely judged. Such a woolly approach disguises a lack of understanding about what has to be done, and some tasks and hazards may not even be identified. It is therefore not surprising that the cost and timescale are underestimated, especially in competitive situations. And, if the purchaser does not probe too deeply — as may be the case — the planning inadequacy is not noticed, especially where the proposal is plausible and specifies an acceptable completion date and cost.

An underlying factor in this scenario is that the reliability of the estimate is related to the depth of the design and plan. Figure 2.3 shows how estimating accuracy improves, as fewer uncertainties remain in the later development stages. (Although the chart suggests equal possibilities of under- and over-estimating, early estimates are usually on the low side.) It is therefore important that estimating should be directed by an experienced manager who can relate the depth of the proposal to the quoted reliability of the estimate.

Some specific causes of poor estimating are given below:

(i) Inadequate design

There may be some ambiguity and uncertainties in the design since it is only at an intermediate level; however, it is not easy to prescribe how much detail is required to reveal clearly all that has to be done in the subsequent development. Some advice is therefore given in the next chapter for management to specify and control the depth of the design work.

(ii) Estimating method

There is, as yet, no standard method for estimating, and the approach often depends

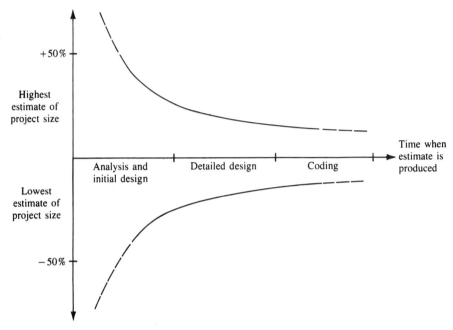

Figure 2.3 How estimating accuracy depends on the state of development

on the experience and preference of the estimator; difficult judgements have to be made about the nature and size of the software and how it can be developed. It is contended throughout this book that such judgements need to be based on a *sound* plan of the project activities — this is the only way to make the estimators think through how the system will actually be produced. And, for the plan to be credible, it also needs to be endorsed by the accountable project manager. However, such a 'planned approach' is more time consuming than other 'short-cut' methods; yet the method is justified (see Chapter 4) and it is strongly advocated, especially for producing a firm estimate of cost and timescale.

(iii) Quantifying the risks

An estimate can only be relied upon if the assessment of the risks and uncertainties is quantified by its impact on cost and timescale. Otherwise, the project manager and directing management do not have a sound basis for their judgement and for setting the budget and objectives for the project. The suggested method is both simple and pragmatic — it assumes that risks can be related to a variance in the costs and timescales of particular activities in the project plan. The uncertainties are then expressed by lower and upper limits of cost and timescale, and the forecasts are accumulated into the overall estimates so that the upper figures include the maximum contingency. The difference between the limits may be substantial, as indicated in Figure 2.3; for example, the lower or optimistic limit may be only

60 per cent of the higher estimate — equivalent to a deviation of plus or minus 25 per cent from a median level.

2.5.1 Summary

The following principles for successful estimating have now emerged:

- There should be a realistic schedule for the work involved in producing the proposal and estimates.
- The architectural design should have 'adequate' depth.
- The project cost and timescale should be based on an implementation plan endorsed by the project manager.
- A range of cost and timescale estimates should be produced to identify the level of risk so that a sound decision can be made in setting the project objectives.

But these principles will not be applied unless the appropriate resources are used to produce the proposal, and this depends on the procurement and resourcing policy, which is considered next.

2.6 Resourcing policy

2.6.1 The need for an operational authority

In constructional projects, it is normal to select the architect first, and the contractor is then appointed at a later date when the quotation is accepted to implement the design. However, the policy for computer systems is more varied. For example, specialised contractors may carry out part, or all, of the design and implementation, with or without competitive tendering; or a large purchasing organisation may use its own resources, possibly in conjunction with those of a contractor. But, in contracting scenarios, the purchaser should have a separate technical or 'operational' authority to work alongside the project manager. This operational manager should be trusted to represent the interests of the purchaser and end-users — in specifying the requirements, planning operational tasks which are outside the scope of the project, and in monitoring the project on behalf of the purchaser.

This two-fold management responsibility is illustrated in Figure 2.4, and it is noteworthy that many projects have failed or have run into severe difficulties because a qualified 'operational authority' did not exist; this will be evident from some of the case studies described in this book.

2.6.2 The project authority

For smaller projects, or those resourced by in-house staff, it is often possible to appoint a single project leader for the entire development process. But this

Figure 2.4 The dual
responsibilities in
launching a project

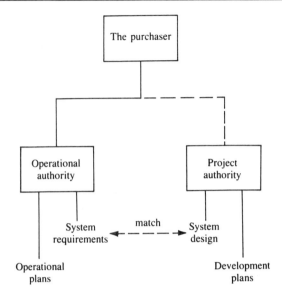

is less likely for a large project where it is difficult to foresee the size and the
hazards at the outset. Furthermore, few people are qualified to lead both design
and implementation tasks for a large project; the creative emphasis in the proposal
phase is markedly different from the tough management challenge of the
implementation task. Contracting firms may also find it difficult to appoint a
'permanent' project manager before the proposal phase when the outcome is
uncertain; and it is very difficult to recruit a project manager if there is any risk
that the development may not proceed after the design phase.

Where the design leader will not also lead the project, the timing of the
appointment of the project manager is crucial. It needs to be early enough for
the manager to under-write the design, especially the strategy for the
implementation. Otherwise, if the project manager is not involved until after the
project is approved, the system design and plan may subsequently have to be
changed to make them viable; and the delay and cost of the belated modifications
may be regarded as a penalty to be paid for the delayed appointment. It may also
be very difficult to make significant changes after the project is committed
contractually. Yet, if the weaknesses are not corrected at the outset, it will be
more difficult to extricate the project at a later time, with an even heavier penalty
in terms of cost and timescale. In any event, the project manager needs to have
exceptional ability to be able to extricate the project from such difficulties. (This
issue is explored further in Chapters 5 and 6.)

It is therefore strongly recommended that the potential manager should be
identified, and be accessible, well before the end of the project phase. And, if
contractors are involved, purchasers are advised to check that the nominated project
manager is qualified and available — and to make this an essential condition for
contractual bidding.

2.6.3 Summary

In the procurement phase, the purchaser is responsible for orchestrating the production of the proposal so that it provides a sound basis for the project decision; this also involves ensuring that the project manager and the (purchaser's) operational manager are both well qualified for the job — and are available before the proposal is approved.

These issues are most important when contractors are involved, particularly if on a competitive basis. (More detailed guidance on procurement policy can be obtained from the *STARTS Purchasers' Handbook*.)

2.7 Using contractors

Since many purchasers do not have adequate in-house skills for a large project, the design and subsequent implementation are often contracted out, usually on a competitive basis. The implications of some different forms of contracting are considered below.

2.7.1 A competitive approach

Competitive bidding aims to provide the purchaser with the 'best' and 'cheapest' solution. It commonly involves evaluating two or more design proposals for implementing the system at a fixed price. Although the proposals should match the purchaser's requirements, any subsequent change entitles the contractor to charge for the extra work; thus the purchaser should take special care to ensure that the requirements are complete and correct, especially if produced by external resources.

Some of the advantages in obtaining a fixed-price implementation are given below:

- It provides some confidence in the contractor's ability to do the job, and some protection for the purchaser against escalating costs and delays.
- The contractor has a strong incentive to achieve the task on time and within budget.

However, competitive bidding also has some limitations, as described below.

2.7.2 Some limitations of competitive bidding

1. Cost. Design proposals for very large projects are so expensive that contractors may be deterred from bidding, especially where scarce resources are required. This problem can be eased if the cost is subsidised by purchasers. However, contractors may still be deterred if the evaluation is to be prolonged — as often occurs — especially since it is difficult to retain key staff on standby after submitting the proposal.
2. High risks. The amount of contingency required to cover the risks and contractual penalties may deter contractors from bidding. High risk for the

contractor is also not in the purchaser's interest; at worst, it may cause the abandonment of the project, or it may provoke the contractor to take negative, defensive action when costs begin to exceed the project budget. For example, effort may be diverted towards opportunities for increasing the charges to the purchaser. Contractual clauses cannot therefore safeguard purchasers against failure or extra expense, and this may include indirect business costs if the project, and the availability of the computer system, is delayed beyond the planned date.

3. Cost-effectiveness of the design. The common practice of initiating the design work, after producing a complete specification of requirements, makes it difficult to achieve the interaction needed for a cost-effective solution. However, some flexibility can be provided in various ways: the requirements may be graded 'essential' and 'desirable'; or selected requirements may be specified only in outline, and contractors asked to propose the details. But such variations do make it rather more difficult and time consuming for the purchaser to compare the different proposals.

2.7.3 Precautions in using contractors

Some dangers are described below. They may be reduced by safeguards in the requirement specification or in the contract, but the actual outcome will depend on the experience, capability and goodwill of both parties.

(i) Lack of a 'total system' approach

The project task should be precisely defined; but it does not normally cover the total system, and other tasks have to be carried out by the purchaser's 'Operational Authority', as indicated in Figure 2.5. However, there is a danger that rigid adherence to the defined responsibilities will create a sort of 'project barrier' with the users; and this will weaken the overall co-ordination of all activities. It is not easy to overcome this problem because commercial pressures restrict flexibility and place over-reliance on the self-sufficiency of each party.

One suggestion for avoiding some conflict and lack of co-operation is to agree that some tasks should involve both parties; for example, joint teams can be

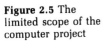

Figure 2.5 The limited scope of the computer project

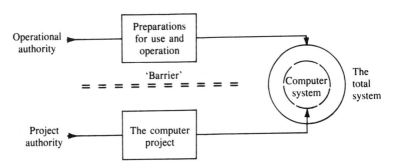

established to train the users and plan the installation, operation and on-going support of the system.

(ii) Impact of changes

During the course of the project, it is usually necessary to make some changes to the requirements in order to correct deficiencies in the specification or to allow for the dynamics of the purchaser's business. Since such changes will be costed on a non-competitive basis, the purchaser should be safeguarded against over-pricing; for example, the contractor should agree to use a defined estimating procedure, based on a detailed plan of the work; there should also be an agreed mark-up for overheads and profit.

Some changes can be very expensive if other work is affected. For example, a belated design change which requires only three man-months of effort may depend on the work of one key person; if the change also delays other project activities by three months, the cost will then escalate to cover the under-utilised staff whose work is delayed.

(iii) Quality

It is inevitable that there will be undetected software defects after the system tests; most of these will emerge as the system is being stretched to cope with the full load. The acceptance criteria should therefore specify a limit to the number of defects which remain to be corrected at the time of acceptance. As a further safeguard, the project authority should be committed to a warranty period for correcting outstanding defects.

Projects are often delayed by poor quality control during the development, and, given the record of many past projects, purchasers should ensure that contractors use good preventive practices to minimise the incidence of defects. (The US Department of Defense standards provide a good illustration of the extent of these constraints, and of the high level of professionalism which is expected of a contractor.)

(iv) On-going maintenance

Most large systems need continuous updating, and software experts who thoroughly understand the developed system must be available on a long-term basis. If the project authority is not to have the on-going role, special arrangements have to be made for training the staff during the project timescale.

2.7.4 Alternative contracting policies

The competitive process may take many forms. There may be two stages: preliminary design studies, which may or may not be competitive, can produce a set of requirements and design strategy; then, after this has been determined, competitive design proposals can be produced. There may even be a further stage for some pioneering systems, where the final selection is made after the short-listed contractors have implemented a pilot system for operational evaluation.

At the other extreme, a trusted contractor may be appointed without a competitive process. The chosen contractor may then produce the detailed requirements as well as the design and project plan. Although such a policy does not obtain a competitive costing, the following benefits counter some of the contracting drawbacks described in the preceding sections:

- There should be close coupling between the requirements specification and the design which should improve the cost-effectiveness of the system and its development.
- The early commitment to a single contractor makes it easier to appoint the project manager during the design phase.
- The contractor's attitude should be flexible and in harmony with that of the purchaser, for example, by assisting the purchaser to prepare for the use, operation and on-going support of the system.

2.7.5   Consortium of contractors

The largest projects need to be resourced by a consortium or a partnership of several contractors. This often applies to projects which require special hardware or communication sub-systems or where other specialised development skills are required. The consortium is usually led by a prime contractor who takes overall responsibility for the development, co-ordinates the sub-contractors and also manages a major part of the project directly.

If software sub-contractors are involved, there should be safeguards against blinkered perspectives, especially where the outputs have to be knitted together to form the overall system. Particular care is needed in specifying the required interfaces between each output and other parts of the system, and in defining measurable criteria for accepting the completed work of each sub-contractor.

2.8   Appraisal of the project proposal

Although the development gradually expands the design through to the working system, there is a major interruption to allow the business decision about the project to be reached. In essence, the basis of the decision is simple — does the design meet the needs of the business, and are the costs and timescale acceptable? But, in practice, the appraisal of competing proposals for a very large project can take several months.

The purchaser has to determine whether the design meets the specified requirements, and whether the project authority has the capability to deliver a sound system. There should also be a careful check that the costing signifies an efficient approach, with acceptable risk. The requirements themselves should also be re-assessed because many projects have run into serious difficulties, and have even failed, because of a belated realisation that the real business need was not being met; some guidelines are given on this subject in the next chapter, along with a review of the design.

From the contractor's standpoint, the directing management needs to be assured that the design and costing are sound, and that there is adequate cover for the risks. The project manager's estimates usually come under pressure in order to minimise a competitive bid. The astute contractor will also reduce the cost by pruning the proposal so that it offers no more than the bare minimum of compliance with the contractual requirements; and the price may be reduced even further if the project is to be a reference for future business.

2.8.1 The scope of the review

Because both purchaser and contractor need a soundly based project with acceptable risks, the review should cover similar ground, as shown below, although some details of the plans and costings in a fixed-price contract will not be revealed to the purchaser.

(i) Compliance with the requirements

The design has to be thoroughly checked to verify that it does meet the requirements, and the purchaser should examine any assertions which are not backed up by evidence. For example, predictions of system performance and reliability are going to be largely theoretical, and they will depend on assumptions about the quality of the design and the subsequent development; they should therefore be carefully probed by technical experts, and this is where the purchaser's 'Operational Authority' is particularly needed to check the contractor's forecasts. (Some typical examples of design weaknesses are examined in the following chapter.)

(ii) Costs

Although the contractor will examine the costing in detail, the purchaser may only see a summarised breakdown of the cost of the project. Nevertheless, the purchaser may be able to deduce more of the cost breakdown by examining the project plan — assuming that the plan is sufficiently detailed and shows the staffing levels.

The purchaser also has to consider other costs which are outside the responsibility of the project. At a physical level, this may include the housing for the computer system and the communication links; there is also the preparatory work for the use of the system, including staff training. However, the major cost is for the on-going operation, use and maintenance of the system; these activities should be included in the project proposal because they are affected by the system design and by its maintainability. The purchaser should also make some provision for changes to the design — because there will be some!

(iii) Risks

Both parties should examine the specified contingencies for risks, and their influence on the cost and timescale limits, as was discussed in Section 2.5. The contractor's assessment will be influenced by commercial considerations and it will be confidential in a fixed-price bid. On the other hand, the purchaser's assessment is limited by what is disclosed in the plan. However, risks are inevitable in large projects; and although some may not be apparent to the purchaser, it is vital that they have been assessed by the contractor; this re-emphasises the dependency on the capability of the contractor.

On the other hand, major problems should be discussed openly, and the contingencies should be apparent within the project plan. In some cases, there may be alternative provisions in the plan where a joint resolution is required at a later date; for example, some novel hardware may not yet have been properly evaluated, or the case for special security software may need further investigation. It may even be sensible, in such cases, to exclude these items from a fixed-price liability so that the later decision is not prejudiced.

(iv) Project capability

A project plan should reveal much about the capability of the project authority; and this can be discerned by management without having to make a detailed technical probe, as demonstrated in Chapter 4. One such appraisal is illustrated in Figure 2.6, which shows how to test the depth and soundness of the plan by whether it includes certain key indicators, such as the following:

• The plan should make provision for a thorough check of the detailed design before it is approved (it is well proven that the cost of correcting defects escalates if they remain until the final tests).
• The final system testing stage is much more difficult to plan than the preceding stages, and at least an outline test plan should be included in the proposal.

Figure 2.6 Some indicators of sound planning

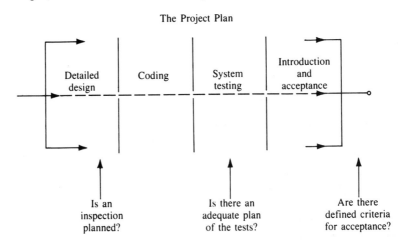

The Project Plan

| Detailed design | Coding | System testing | Introduction and acceptance |

Is an inspection planned?   Is there an adequate plan of the tests?   Are there defined criteria for acceptance?

- Although it is not easy to define precise criteria for the end of the project, any vagueness can affect the cost and timescale and cause subsequent controversy.

Provisions such as these in the project proposal should give the purchaser some assurance of the capability of the contractors; however, such an appraisal at a management level must also be supplemented by a detailed technical examination of the design and plans.

2.8.2   Summary

It has been shown that much of the appraisal is related to the project plan. This issue will now be followed up in the next section to investigate how management can ensure that a sound plan will be produced.

2.9   Orchestrating the work

The manner of reviewing the project proposal depends on whether the design proposal is separated from that of the planning and costing. The following examples illustrate some variations in the approach.

2.9.1   The one-part proposal

Here, the design is combined with the project plan and costing to form a composite proposal. For very large projects such an approach is handicapped by the large scale and complexity of the proposal; for example, just one amendment to the design can have a widespread effect on both design and plan. Furthermore, the time needed to review the proposal may be so prolonged that a contractor is unable to retain some of the staff to work on the subsequent project.

2.9.2   The two-part proposal

In this approach, the design proposal is submitted in advance of the final plan and costing. This allows the design process to serve as a preliminary test in competitive contracts; then only the preferred design solutions are included in a short list of contractors who tender the firm project plans and costs.

There can be many variations in a two-part submission. For example, the design proposal may include an outline project plan and timescale, possibly with a budgetary costing; alternatively, the design proposal may only include the implementation strategy and a rough indication of the possible range of cost and timescale.

2.9.3   Summary

In the author's experience, the project plan is often given inadequate emphasis in producing the proposal, and insufficient time and effort is allocated to the task.

Therefore, irrespective of the manner of presenting the proposal, it is strongly recommended that the 'what' (the design task) is separated from the 'how' (the planning task). By separating the two tasks, each can be carried out by staff who have the appropriate qualifications; this should ensure that those who produce the project plan are also made accountable for it. Such an arrangement also allows the planners to carry out a check and balance of the design, especially on the implications for the implementation task (this is described in Chapter 4).

The recommended manner of orchestrating the production of the project proposal is shown in Figure 2.7; this also indicates the other tasks involved in forming the complete system proposal — these are assumed to be the direct responsibility of the purchaser.

Figure 2.7
Orchestrating the resources and tasks for producing the project proposal

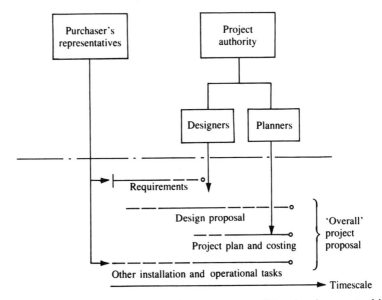

This approach leads to the following summary of the development which is assumed in this book:

Phase	Decision/product
1. Feasibility study	Intention to develop system with terms of reference for design study
2. Project proposal:	
• requirements analysis	Approve design subject to confirmation of
• architectural design	cost/timescale
• project plan	Commit to development with budgets and
• operational plan	plans
3. Project implementation	Acceptance of system

These phases are examined separately in the subsequent chapters. It is perhaps of interest to make a comparison with the practice in other industries. For example, in construction projects, the architect produces the design to meet the purchaser's requirements; the design is then submitted to builders for their plans and estimates and the purchaser can then authorise the constructional work. This principle, of distinguishing between suitability of solution and affordable cost of implementation, is reflected in the suggested approach for launching a computer project. However, even if a different approach is used which does not distinguish between design and planning tasks, many of the guidelines in the following chapters should still be applicable.

3 Analysis and design

3.1 Introduction

The proposed system is conceived during the initial stage of the development process, and the main aim of this chapter is to explore the answer to the following question:

> How can management ensure that the design of the computer system can be relied upon to meet the stated requirement?

In answering the question, we will consider how management can effectively direct the design task without having detailed technical knowledge of the design process. The main focus will be on how the design will perform as an operational system, and whether it can be reliably implemented. And it will be shown that management can detect design weaknesses and improvement possibilities by concentrating on the effect of the design on the users and implementers, rather than on the design mechanism. The technical processes are therefore only mentioned briefly, and it is assumed that this work is led by a qualified senior designer or design manager.

(A more detailed survey of design methods and technologies is given by Macro and Buxton 1987, and some detailed check lists for managing the activity are given in the STARTS Developers' Guide and the US Department of Defense Standards.)

The scope of the design is assumed to cover a new system, including new hardware as well as the bespoke software. Although the project ends after the introduction and proving of the operational system, the on-going operation and maintenance of the system are also briefly considered since they make a substantial contribution to the overall life-time cost of the system.

The basic appreciation of the analysis and design task given in the next three sections is intended to provide a background for the subsequent management guidelines.

3.2 An outline of the task

The design process may begin in different ways, but because it often takes several months to design a large system, some form of preliminary study is usually carried out to determine the broad nature of a feasible system which meets the business requirement. As these studies vary so much in scope, they are not considered in this book, although their importance is acknowledged, especially in defining the terms of reference for the design and planning work.

The design work is usually divided up into two inter-related stages: first, a detailed analysis and specification of what is required from the system; and, second, the design of the computer system which meets the requirements.

The requirements provide the foundation for the design work: they define the information processes to be carried out by the system, known as the functionality; they specify the data required to support the functions; and they prescribe the operational and technical characteristics, such as the capacity and reliability of the system. The design proposal responds with a specification of how the requirements will be met, and also provides an architectural blueprint of the system. The combination of the design and requirement specifications then provides the firm baseline for the project — firm in the sense that it should only be changed by agreement of both purchaser and project authority.

The requirements analysis and the design work are inter-related since it is pointless to produce requirements for an impractical or unaffordable system; furthermore, as will be demonstrated, some requirements cannot be prescribed, let alone finalised, until the design has evolved. However, the interaction may be somewhat restricted by the commercial constraints of competitive contracting, as described in the preceding chapter.

3.3 The problems

Management should aim to avoid problems such as those illustrated below:

A large system was designed as an upgraded replacement of an existing one. Apart from the need for more capacity and some new functions, it was important that the new system should suffer very few operational interruptions through hardware failures; consequently, dual processors were specified so that a failure of one processor would not cause a prolonged breakdown. A contractor was chosen to produce a design proposal and an implementation plan to match the purchaser's requirements.

Although the project plan appeared to be sound, the operating implications had not been fully reflected in either requirements or design. This emerged during the detailed design stage; at that time, the purchaser's technical staff received unsatisfactory answers from the project team about how the system would react to certain operational failures — especially how service could be speedily restored. For example, despite the provision of dual processors, it was found that the operators had to carry out a very complicated and hazardous recovery operation when one

Case history 1

processor failed. After reviewing the design, it was decided that the recovery procedures must be made easier and safer; and it then transpired that the re-design work would delay the project by about one year and increase the project cost by 50 per cent.

Eventually, agreement to the changes was reached, and the project was satisfactorily completed — but both contractor and purchaser had to share the excess costs, and the business suffered by having to tolerate the current inadequate system for much longer than had been anticipated.

The following lessons can be learned from this episode:

- The operational requirements should be defined in practical terms which state the impact on the operational service — and they should be specified by staff who are experienced in the operation of similar systems.
- There should be close liaison between the analysts and designers to ensure that the requirements, especially the operational requirements, are interpreted correctly.
- The design should be carefully checked by the analysts who specify the requirements.

In addition to these specific safeguards, common problems arising from an inadequate design can be categorised as listed below:

1. System performance. The performance of the operational system may not match the design prediction; for example, its response to users' requests may be too slow, or the system may not be able to cope with the peak load, or there is excessive disruption caused by teething problems. Such weaknesses are often not detected until the final testing stage, or even later, during the operation of the system.
2. Cost-effectiveness. A poorly designed system may be inefficient in its use of computing time and hardware, and be difficult or costly to maintain. Although such design defects may be exposed by comparing the costs of competitive bids, some may be obscured because the proposal costs have been under-estimated; and, in this event, although the purchaser may be protected in a fixed-price contract against excess hardware costs, there may be excessive operating or maintenance costs which are outside the contractual liability of the project authority.
3. Implementation cost and timescale. There may be insufficient depth in the design to produce a reliable forecast of the development cost and timescale. And a complex design structure can cause a troublesome and protracted introduction of the system, especially if the design does not allow the development to be phased into sufficiently small sub-systems.
4. Compliance with requirements. It is difficult to verify whether a theoretical design specification does meet the requirements, especially when there are pioneering aspects; hence, special techniques may have to be used, such as

the construction of a prototype model of part of the system to check critical aspects of the design.

Suggestions, made later in the chapter, should help management recognise and avoid some of the problems listed above. However, the best safeguard is to select qualified analysts and designers who can be relied upon; and an indication of their role is given in the following outline of the task.

3.4   Analysing the requirements

The requirements are considered in the following two categories:

1. The functional requirements which define the structure of the system, and prescribe 'what' information processes and results are needed.
2. The non-functional or technical requirements which specify the performance of the system and the constraints for its development and operation — they indicate 'how well' the system must perform its processing tasks in the given environment.

Each of these categories is considered below, but whilst the distinction is fundamental in helping to identify the requirements, the dividing line is somewhat flexible and some items may be placed in either category.

3.4.1   The functional requirements

The functional requirements specify details of the following components of an information system:

*   Input data. These describe the physical form and composition of each item, with all the possible variations which might arise in practice, including the maximum range of values to be assigned to an item.
*   Output results. These are specified in the same manner as for the input data.
*   Record files. These cover the different types of data to be stored for reference, where each item is specified in the same detail as for the input and output.
*   Processes. These describe how the input and record data are to be manipulated to produce the required results; this includes specifying the sequence and parallelism of the processes, together with all exceptional procedures for dealing with abnormal situations; for example, the action to be taken if the input data is incorrect, or to prevent unauthorised access to the file records.

An indication of some problems and precautions which may arise in producing the requirements listed above is given below.

1. Errors. Extreme thoroughness is necessary because any inaccuracy or ambiguity is likely to cause a design error. And the time and effort of special precautions will definitely pay dividends; it has been amply demonstrated in several references (including Boehm 1981 and Kitchenham *et al.* 1986) that the cost of correcting errors escalates greatly if they are left until later

stages of the project. And one of the most cost effective precautions is a thorough inspection of the completed specifications by both technical specialists and user representatives.

2. Production method. The analysis process may follow one of the standard disciplined procedures (known as methodologies); these organise the work by structuring it into a series of steps, and use a standard format for presenting the results. Such methods aim to reduce the complexity of the task and improve the detailed accuracy; and the structured approach also helps to schedule and control the work. However, care is needed that emphasis on the detailed accuracy of the work does not obscure the real needs of the business; and the analysis work should be phased so that the main requirements are considered and approved before the details are defined.

3. Users' involvement. A common difficulty in specifying functional requirements is that users do not find it easy to visualise their information needs in a theoretical context. This dilemma is sometimes resolved by the analysts themselves who take the initiative by making suggestions to the users — to meet the oft-heard plea of 'I will know what I want when I see it.' However, this may leave gaps if the analysts lack detailed knowledge of the business, and strong efforts should always be made to obtain the active involvement of the end-users.

4. Presentation. Although the users should check the specifications, it is always difficult to validate lengthy written specifications. To make the requirements more intelligible, they should be compartmentalised with copious use of charts and illustrations. However, this may not occur unless management gives some prior direction about the format to be used for the results. It may also be advisable to devise a practical demonstration, using a mini-computer system, to display some features, especially of the screen formats (this is described in Section 3.6).

Because the cost of the system increases as the requirements are extended, management should discourage the inclusion of 'desirables' which are not essential.

3.4.2   *The technical requirements — an overview*

These requirements are concerned with 'how well' the system will perform, and with constraints about how it is to be developed, installed, operated and serviced. The requirements must aim to ensure that the purchaser has a satisfactory system over its expected life-time. And, because some constraints are difficult to define and measure, such as reliability, special care is needed so that the achievement can be objectively verified.

Aids for producing these specifications do not exist to the same extent as for the functional requirements; nor is there so much guidance in the literature. In practice, therefore, the technical requirements often materialise as a rather disorganised set of sundry items with no clear framework. Consequently, a perspective viewpoint is given below to help management recognise what should be specified. (Other more detailed guidelines are given in the STARTS Purchasers' Handbook and in the US Department of Defense Standards.)

The requirements are considered in the following three categories:

1. System capability. This covers the capacity, reliability and performance of the operational system, which are largely reflected in the architectural design of the system and, also, partly in the implementation.
2. Implementation. This covers constraints on the cost, timescale and quality of the products to be produced and installed. In practice these constraints are often skimped; possibly because there is no generally accepted standard, or perhaps because it is felt that a purchaser should not dictate how a contractor does his job.
3. Operation. This covers constraints on the environment and on the operating and maintenance resources for the life-time support of the system.

The influence of these requirements on the design and planning tasks is shown in Figure 3.1. Thus the requirements for system capability combine with the functional requirements to affect the design architecture. The other technical requirements, the implementation and operational constraints, influence the project plans as well as parts of the design. Each category of requirement is considered in more detail in the following sections.

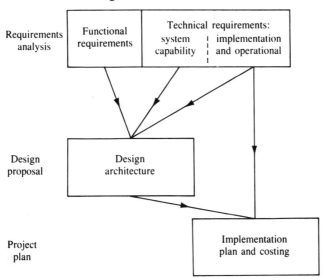

Figure 3.1 The main interfaces between the requirements, design and project plan

3.4.3 Capability requirements

Some specific examples are given below:

1. System performance. For transaction systems, the required response time should be specified for the peak loading of each type of terminal operation. The extent of a transaction should also be precisely defined; for example,

does it start at the beginning or end of the keyboard input and output response? For batch processing, the start and deadline completion times are specified, for example 'delivery notes must be available before 8 a.m.'.

2. System capacity. It is necessary to specify this in some way which ensures that there is sufficient hardware capacity to cope with the peak workload and future expansion. (This is illustrated in Section 3.6.) The requirement should cover each hardware sub-system, including the communication lines and the storage of data records.

3. Operational reliability. The following is an example of part of a requirement specification:

    *   short term: there should be no more than one system failure per 100 hours of operation, and this should not cause more than thirty minutes' unavailability of the operational system ('availability' has to be specifically defined).

    *   long term: there should be no more than five system failures in any consecutive period of 1000 hours of operation, during which the total amount of unavailability of the overall system should be less than two hours.

        Additional specifications are required for failures which do not disrupt the overall system but which degrade its operation; this should cover failure of a hardware sub-system, terminals or of a particular application. These partial system failures may be represented by allocating a weighting factor to a sub-system. This can then reflect its contribution to the overall operation; for example, two successive interruptions which disable half of the system for thirty minutes may be counted as an overall system failure of thirty minutes.

4. Interface requirements. Standards should be defined for all interfaces between the system and its users, such as screen formats and terminal facilities.

5. Local constraints. These may include the need for compatibility with existing systems.

Increasing the scope or stringency of the above requirements adds to the cost of the project, for example the need for a very high reliability or speed of response. It is therefore not only necessary to define requirements completely and precisely, they also need to be limited to the essential. An indication of the cost escalation of requirements in the original specification is shown in Figure 3.2. However, the costs will be even higher if requirements are not precisely specified until late in the project. For example, the lack of measurable criteria for reliability may cause very costly modifications if this is only tackled after the system has been introduced, as is also illustrated in Figure 3.2.

3.4.4 *Implementation requirements*

The system development plan needs to be under-written by a technical expert acting on behalf of the purchaser, and some constraints should be imposed on

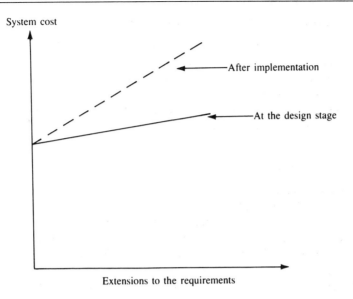

Figure 3.2 The cost of increasing requirements

System cost

After implementation

At the design stage

Extensions to the requirements

the designers and planners, as indicated below. (These issues will also be followed up in the next chapter, on project planning.)

1. Quality. If the quality of the software development is poor, the operational reliability will be unsatisfactory, and the implementation timescale will also be delayed . Bearing in mind the poor history of many past projects, good quality cannot be taken for granted, and yet safeguards have been somewhat neglected by purchasers; hence some mandatory requirements should be imposed on contractors to ensure that there will be tight quality control. (Some detailed guidelines are given in the following two chapters.)
2. Installation. Constraints have to be specified for issues such as the location and housing of the hardware, any communication network, the retention of existing facilities, and any constructional work.
3. Preparation for use and maintenance. The purchaser should seek assurances that project activities will be co-ordinated with any other related tasks and the operational preparations — these may be carried out by the purchaser or other contractors. This re-emphasises the importance of a 'total system' approach. The development plans should also demonstrate that the system can be maintained in a cost-effective manner over its life-time.
4. System introduction. Any target timescale for achieving full use of the system should be subject to a defined and practical strategy for introducing the system. (This topic is explored later, in Section 3.7.)
5. Management control and commercial constraints. These include progress reviews, procedures for changes, progress milestones, acceptance criteria, payments and penalties.

3.4.5   *Operational requirements*

Because some of these requirements influence the system design, the purchaser needs expert advice, possibly from the operational authority, to produce a specification which is comprehensive. This is particularly important if the project authority is not to be involved in the aftercare of the system.

A brief indication of some operational requirements is given below, together with an outline of the basic tasks.

(i)   *Operating*

The operating staff produce the daily work schedules, control the work flow and deal with queries and problems raised by the users; they also control the internal housekeeping of the system, especially the safe-keeping of the magnetic storage files. The staffing level depends on the need for on-site attendance at the computer centres, and on shift working; and specialist(s) will be required to control the performance of a communications network.

The operators should be good problem solvers. Although technical defects are corrected by the engineering and software staff, the operators take the first-line action to rapidly restore the service after a disruption. Bearing in mind the impact of a few lost minutes of operation of a powerful computer, much depends on the operators' ability to work speedily and under pressure — this emphasises the need for collaboration with the project authority in the careful selection and training of the staff, and in the provision of aids for the tasks.

The purchaser should therefore request the submission of a training plan for the end-users and system operators, and also an outline of the operating manuals. These manuals are usually produced much later, and yet they are a vital part of the project foundations: they demonstrate the usability of the system; they also provide a practical validation of much of the design, for example by defining procedures for dealing with data and operator errors.

(ii)   *Software support*

The term 'software support' is used to cover enhancements of the software as well as correction of software defects and housekeeping routines. The support policy needs to be clearly specified because some activities may disrupt the operational service. For example, after software changes have been thoroughly tested in an off-line test bed, they are usually applied in batches as periodical re-issues; these should occur overnight or at weekends or during other quiet periods. There will also be some on-line support activity in the housekeeping tasks for preserving the integrity of files; and these should be scheduled for times when the operational service is least disturbed.

The requirements which relate to the support resources depend on the chosen staffing policy. Any uncertainty about the staffing arrangements has to be resolved with the contractor; for example, if the on-going support is not to be provided by the project, the contractor may be asked for a transition plan, including staff training, to achieve a smooth handover to the support authority.

(iii) Hardware maintenance

This is usually provided by the relevant manufacturer or by another specialist contractor; it may also cover the proprietary system software which is linked with the hardware. Apart from examining the provisions and cost of the service, the purchaser should check that spares and maintenance cover will be available throughout the envisaged life-time of the system.

3.5   The design proposal

Because the design of a large system is such a highly technical and creative task, it is difficult for management to be assured that the design is sound and cost-effective. It may therefore be helpful to see the key features in perspective, as indicated below:

The design proposal consists of the following:

- the design architecture, which describes the system, its components and how they will work together;
- specifications showing how the relevant requirements are met for implementing and operating the system.

The architecture provides a theoretical model of the operational system, and also a constructional blueprint for its development. The designers may be assisted by using a standard design technique — related to the type of system being developed. The design technique may also be combined with the use of a formal methodology for expressing the specifications, as for the requirements analysis. Such methods reduce the complexity of the task by structuring the process and by using a standard format for the specifications.

The design may proceed in a variety of ways, but preliminary versions should evaluate possible alternatives — and assess any major hazards and cost/benefit trade-offs on non-essential requirements. After some iteration of this preliminary work, it should be possible to select the preferred design, the major hardware units and other bought-in components.

The design includes several types of component, both hardware and software; and these interact to form the operational system with the required functions, performance and capacity. This combination is illustrated in Figure 3.3 and each type of system component is considered below.

3.5.1   Hardware and communications equipment

Specifications are produced of the bought-in units, their inter-connections and man—machine interfaces, spares provisions, procurement details, costs and

Figure 3.3 The
composition of the
system architecture

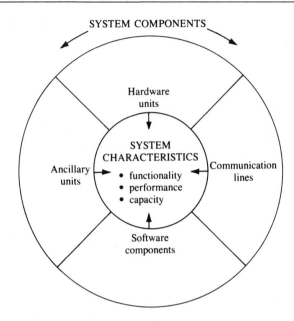

timescales. The products should be justified by their cost-effectiveness, and any risks should be highlighted, together with proposals for their reduction. This should include the precautions and plans for dealing with a special hardware development, or modification, or the pioneering use of some equipment; for example, this might relate to a novel approach for controlling the traffic load in a communication network.

3.5.2   Software specifications

The software design needs to satisfy both functional and technical requirements, as indicated below:

(i) Compliance with the functional requirements

This is the main challenge — specifying a cost-effective set of software in adequate depth to ensure that it meets the requirement. And since the software architecture is only at an intermediate level, management should take special precautions, as outlined in Section 3.6, to ensure that an adequate depth of design is produced.

Although the correctness of the design should be carefully cross-checked, it may be necessary to validate a critical or pioneering aspect in a practical manner by developing a 'prototype' mini-system (powerful 'macro' languages may allow such a prototype to be produced relatively quickly).

In addition to the functional processes, the specifications should cover the following:

- the data and results, including the man—machine interfaces and screen formats at the terminals;
- the organisation of the data-base to show the file layouts and arrangements for describing and accessing the data;
- other system interfaces with the operating system software, retained applications and communications networks;
- all exceptional conditions, including security against unauthorised access.

(ii) Software compliance with the technical requirements

Just three aspects, which depend on the software design, are singled out for illustration because they have often caused problems in past projects:

1. Software defects are the main cause of system unreliability, and a target should be set for the number of errors to emerge in the initial period of operation, together with a time limit for their correction. Such a specification should also strengthen the purchaser's confidence in the reliability of the completed system — and in the capability of the contractor (see also Section 3.7).
2. The system capacity depends on software design limits for the size of files and tables; for example, there will be a maximum number of terminals which can be connected. And, if the limits are not fully specified, a major problem may not surface until late in the project, or even in live running, when a catastrophic operational failure occurs because the system is over-stretched.
3. The safe housekeeping of the operational system depends on adequate design features for the maintenance of the system. And, even if the detailed requirements are not fully specified by the purchaser, the designers should be expected to apply good professional standards which keep the system in a safe and usable state; for example, arrangements should be made to transfer data from working files before they become full.

3.5.3   Ancillary products

Examples of some software products which may have to be produced, and which are sometimes overlooked are as follows:

- 'drivers': to link the application programs with some hardware peripherals and communication lines;
- 'system software': to augment any inadequacies in the standard software provided by the hardware manufacturer;
- 'tailor made' software: to control the loading of the initial data records before live running can commence.
- operational housekeeping facilities and procedures: such as those for the periodical archiving of data, to avoid the overloading of the storage devices.
- test routines: to confirm the correct operation of the system, particularly after any repair work to the hardware or changes to the software.

3.5.4 Overall system capacity and performance

A forecast of the system performance is obtained by the so-called 'sizing' exercise. This is a mathematical technique for predicting the hardware capacity which will accommodate the software programs and data, and deliver the required performance. The sizing result should predict the following:

- how the software, both programs and data, can be organised and accommodated or 'mapped' in the hardware;
- how the peak workload can be accommodated;
- the performance levels for terminal response times and batch processing schedules;
- how the system can meet the reliability requirements, including its ability to avoid or recover from catastrophic failures, having regard to the spare hardware which is to be provided (see Section 3.7).

It may be found during the design process that a workload requirement has not been specified clearly. This sometimes arises for an *ad hoc* application where the purchaser cannot easily forecast the extent of the load; for example, queries which interrogate data files. But the purchaser should be pinned down to a commitment; and any such ambiguity should be removed by specifying the maximum load of user input; this will then avoid controversy if the operational system becomes over-loaded.

3.6 Management direction and appraisal

Management will be involved in formulating the particular design strategy, and in organising and scheduling the design activities. However, the extent of this influence will vary, depending on the nature of the system, the technical capability of the manager and that of the leading designers. These technical aspects of the role are not covered in this chapter since they relate to the particular situation. Instead, the emphasis is on the more general directives and precautions which apply to all systems; for example, to ensure that the design can be relied upon to meet the requirements, and to provide adequate briefs for the planning and estimating work and for the subsequent development.

The guidelines on direction, given below, describe some controls to be applied before the work commences and during interim reviews; these are followed by suggested appraisals of the completed design. But one particular appraisal — of the introduction of the system — is considered separately and in more depth in Section 3.7.

3.6.1 Management direction

(i) Staffing

The vital task is to ensure that the designers are selected with the correct skills to match the nature of the envisaged system — remember that it is their efforts which will largely determine the cost-effectiveness of the system. And, even with a strong technical leader, the creative nature of the work means that the staff have to be able to work with little technical direction. These designers should also be involved in the subsequent project — to provide some in-built accountability for the quality and effectiveness of their design; otherwise, the staff should at least be accessible for clarifying any issues.

(ii) The work schedule and management reviews

The schedule for the design process should be endorsed by the designers themselves so that they are motivated to achieve the task within the planned timescale. The staff should also be briefed about the purpose and scope of progress reviews, especially the final appraisal; such advanced notice should help to make the reviews much more effective than otherwise.

(iii) Design structure and standards

The design methodology should be suitable for the particular type of system, and should make adequate allowance for the staff learning curve since this has caused serious delays in some projects. The format for presenting the design should also be prescribed so that it will be intelligible, both to management and to the purchaser's representatives.

(iv) Depth of the software design

A large system is dissected, first into sub-systems and then into lower levels of 'components' until the programs are specified. It is the lowest of these levels which determines the reliability of estimating, and yet this may not be sufficiently detailed unless some directives are given to the designers, such as the following:

- All design components immediately above the module level are to be specified in a defined level of detail.
- All modules are to be identified, and outline flow charts should clarify the functions.
- Module functions are to be specified in detail for 'critical' modules — those which have a major impact on the performance of the system.

However, there is often pressure, where the proposal timescale is tight, to leave the design at some higher level than suggested above. In such cases, the criteria should only be relaxed if management is confident that the level of the design is adequate; and management's judgement should take account of the views of the staff who will have to expand the design — are they confident about carrying out the task in a prescribed timescale?

(v) Preparatory brief for the programmers

This should describe what work has to be done, including a forecast of the effort required to carry out the detailed design work. The forecast is also a check on the design depth; for example, if as much as six months of effort is needed for the detailed design of one component, this is an indication that some further expansion is needed.

The design structure affects the assembly and test of the overall system; therefore the test strategy should be outlined at this time since some projects have experienced great difficulty in getting the constituent programs to work together. Any special test tools or aids should also be specified.

(vi) Inspection of the design

Arrangements should be made for a stringent review of the design to minimise the number of residual errors and omissions.

3.6.2 Appraisal of the software design

For management to assess the need for design changes, it needs to understand any design weaknesses in the context of the overall architecture. But a clear presentation of the design may not happen naturally, and it is suggested that managers should obtain an early view so that they can evolve their understanding before the design is finalised. This may involve several presentations by the designers until the managers understand the key issues; and experience has shown that management may need to persist with these sessions, often to the exasperation of some designers who find simple explanations rather irksome! Such presentations are not only catalysts for communication between management and designers about the risks — they also reveal much about the capability of the designers.

Figure 3.4 gives an indication of a simple presentation for management which describes the system in the following two dimensions;

(a) firstly, the constructional blueprint of the hierarchical structure of the system components, indicating the amount of development and how it is to be organised;

(b) secondly, the functional outline of how the system will work in operation — this is traced through a flow diagram of the main functions and their interaction with data files.

3.6.3 Appraisal of the hardware and physical aspects

The presentation of the physical components of the system should allow management to assess the main information flow through the hardware, to and from the end-users. Some suggestions for probing the cost-effectiveness of the hardware are given below:

• What are the pros and cons of alternative hardware products?
• How much of the main processor capacity is used at times of peak loading, and is there adequate margin for possible load surges? (An example is given later in this section, see p. 42.)

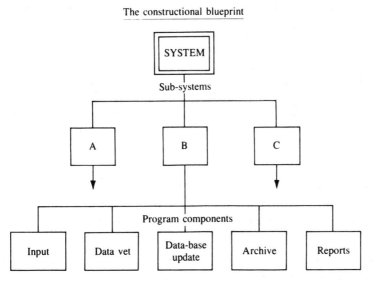

The constructional blueprint

Figure 3.4 A two-fold
presentation of a
system outline

The functional outline of sub-system 'B'

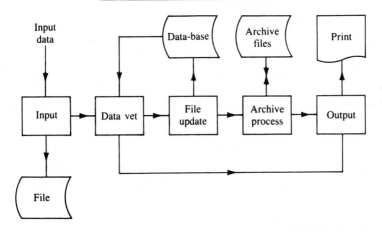

- What 'trade-offs' of hardware capacity and cost can be made by relaxing some requirements?
- What is the extra hardware cost for the envisaged future modifications, enhancements and extra load? Particular attention should be paid to any unit which is not easily expandable, especially if it is 'top of the range'.
- What are the practical implications of extending the capacity? For example, will the operation of the system have to be interrupted for a prolonged period?
- Do the layout diagrams of the equipment indicate that there is adequate physical access and sufficient space for later expansion?
- The plans of any new building works or other special constructional activity should be checked.

3.6.4 *Examples of some typical design hazards*

Although the complete design proposal will be large and technically complex, some useful probes can be made by management, even if it does not have an in-depth understanding of the technical aspects. The following examples are of vulnerable aspects which can escalate the cost or cause major problems. These reviews should also strengthen the overall impression of the proposal and of the designers' capabilities. And, even announcing the intention to hold these reviews is valuable; it encourages the designers to be thorough, and to be prepared to justify the quality of their designs. The subjects covered are as follows:

- ease of usability, particularly for terminal operators;
- the practicality of operating the computer system;
- the relative cost-effectiveness of the different operational applications;
- the accuracy of the projected size and cost of the system;
- whether the design complies with all requirements.

It should be noted that these issues, and others, can also be examined, in depth, by a dedicated 'audit' team who query the designers and report their findings.

(i) Usability

Management should verify for itself how the more important and common transactions will work; in a commercial application, these may include key customer services, order processing and certain management reports. The review can involve a practical presentation of the data and results to simulate the precise manner in which they will appear to the user; this can be set up by a simple computer program which presents data, such as a sales order and a sales analysis, on a computer screen.

It is also important to assess the impact on the business operations if and when the system is unavailable for any reason; for example, how the essential operations can be continued during a breakdown, and the effect on the business and end-users.

(ii) Operability

This can be a question and answer check that the operation of the computer system will be safe and practical; and it is particularly important if the project authority does not have an on-going responsibility. Possible questions are as follows:

- What is the regular operational housekeeping of the system, how much time is required in each day and week, and how will the operational service be affected?
- How are software corrections and upgrades applied and how will the service be affected?
- What are the recovery processes to deal with some possible hardware, software and data errors?

- How will the complete library of discs and tapes be made accessible and yet be safeguarded against damage?
- How will the operating staff be obtained and trained?
- What routine maintenance is required for the hardware and how will this affect the service?

(iii) The relative cost-effectiveness of applications

This can be roughly gauged by examining how much central computing resource is used for the main applications. Figure 3.5 shows how the resource used by the main applications in a commercial system can be shown as a proportion of the total amount of power available over a given period. Then, if the proportion for any particular application is considered to be excessive in relation to its value, a more economical design may be investigated. However, in such a case, a further analysis should show the marginal cost at the time when the application is run. For example, a large amount of computer time may be affordable at 'off-peak' times, when the system is lightly loaded.

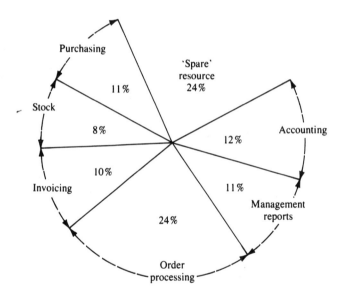

Figure 3.5 Analysing the computing resource for a simple commercial application

(iv) Hardware capacity and operational scheduling

The loading of the computer processor can be displayed graphically, as shown in Figure 3.6. This highlights the key loading patterns: the peak load on a typical day and the highest load on the system at any time. The graph also shows how the hardware has to cope with the peak workload, as opposed to the average level. And, if the peak to average ratio is high, it means that the hardware is relatively

Figure 3.6 A profile
of the system loading

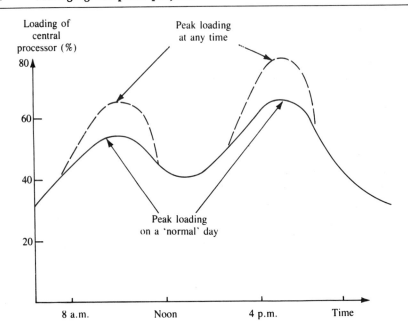

expensive because much of its capacity is rarely used — only for the peak period. In this case, reducing the peak levels may reduce the hardware cost substantially, although this involves changing either the loading or the work scheduling.

These charts need to be interpreted carefully. For example, a peak-hour level of work is a coarse measure. It is the average during that hour; the actual load fluctuates above and below that level. Therefore, provision should be made so that the minute-by-minute variations do not over-load the system; this is why the peak-hour load should occupy less than 100 per cent of the hardware capacity, so that sufficient margin exists to cope with the short-duration peaks. If the purchaser expresses the requirement in peak-hour terms, the project authority should obtain some clarification, either by quantifying the short-term peaks, or by specifying the 'spare' processor capacity above the peak-hour level — possibly around 30 or 40 per cent of the total.

Although sizing only gives a theoretical projection with limited accuracy, an experienced specialist should be able to gauge the uncertainties and predict the risk of a hardware shortfall. More reliable forecasting requires a 'benchmark' test, which runs a critical part of the system on a computer; but this is expensive and time consuming, and may be restricted to projects where novel or unknown hardware is being used or where the performance is critical.

One contingency against under-sizing is to assume that part of the software can be re-designed after it has been tested in order to make it more streamlined. But it is often difficult, and very time consuming, to achieve significant savings after the teething problems and obvious inefficiencies have been corrected; and staff often make optimistic forecasts of what may be achieved. Generally, the most cost-effective contingency for any shortfall of capacity is to provide extra hardware — assuming that the extension is fairly straightforward.

Requirement specification (paragraph ref.)	Design specifications						
	Module A1	A2	A3		Module B1	B2	
1.1			$\checkmark$				
1.2	$\checkmark$						
1.3		$\checkmark$					
.							
.							
.							
2.1						$\checkmark$	
2.2					$\checkmark$		
.							
.							
.							
n.1							
.							
.							
n.m							

Figure 3.7 A cross-reference check of design compliancy

(v) Final compliancy check

The completeness of the design may be checked by a matrix which relates each requirement to the corresponding item in the design proposal, as indicated in Figure 3.7.

3.7   The reliability of the operational system

The design affects the introduction of the system in various ways, for example in determining the phasing of the development and introduction of the system. The design also influences the resilience of the system — its ability to recover from faults without disrupting the operational service — and this affects the operational reliability. All these aspects are considered below.

3.7.1   The introduction of the system

Investigating how the system will be launched into live running is a valuable exercise for exposing much about the practicality of the design. For example, joint studies with the users into how the system and data load will be expanded should highlight the precautions to allow for teething problems, both of the system and of the users. The need for such an appraisal is illustrated below.

A large project was scheduled to be completed in eighteen months following production of the design architecture. The completion date was set by allowing an arbitrary period of two months for the introduction of the system after system testing;   **Case history 2** it was considered that this interval was sufficient to achieve a 'satisfactory' working level of the system, and this would then signify the end of the project.

Although the system test was completed on schedule, the introduction of the system had to be abandoned at the first attempt because of a serious design weakness. It was then decided that, in addition to correcting the defect, the system test should be made more stringent to detect other defects. As a final precaution, the introduction plan was phased so as to stagger the impact of the full data load.

About six weeks later, and after the re-test, the system was successfully introduced. The teething problems gradually diminished until the project manager felt that the system was sufficiently reliable to take the full load. However, in the meantime, other difficulties had arisen because the users were struggling with their own teething problems; and this enforced a slow-down in the take-on of the data load. Eventually, the end of the project was reached — eight months late.

The delay caused much extra cost for both contractor and purchaser since staff had to be retained throughout, and the delay also adversely affected the purchaser's business.

The following lessons emerge from this experience:

• Vague criteria, such as 'satisfactory running' for the end of a project, imply insufficient thought about the final testing of the system, and can cause conflict about the project completion. (Further details about the acceptance criteria are discussed in Chapter 4.)
• Both parties should recognise that it takes a substantial period of time, after completing the system tests, before the system can run with a full load.
• The introductory strategy should be formed jointly by purchaser and designers to take account of business constraints, such as the learning curve of the end-users and the need for the system to become sufficiently stable.

We will now examine more deeply the issues to be considered by management when applying the above lessons.

3.7.2 *Dependencies on the user*

Apart from the danger of technical teething problems, rapid expansion of the system may over-stretch the capability of the business, especially if there are new business procedures. The loading should be expanded, step by step, in a series of controllable increments; this may bring in successive groups of end-users and terminals.

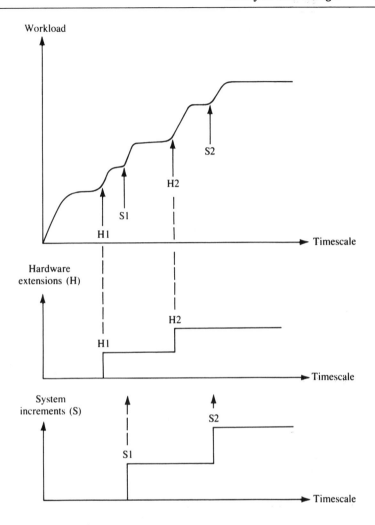

Figure 3.8 Planning
the introduction of
the system

During the initial period, some urgent software changes are often required; for example, a particular user procedure might be excessively cumbersome and prone to error, or extra information may have to be inserted in a management report. However, apart from minor enhancements which can be combined with error corrections, unplanned changes disrupt and delay the completion of the project. And although the purchaser may be responsible for the direct cost of the software changes, delays escalate the staffing costs for both parties. Hence the loading schedule should envisage such eventualities and allow for some agreed level of change.

A plan for the introductory period may take the form shown in Figure 3.8, and this should make allowance for the users' teething problems following each change to the system. The plan will also need to take account of the technical teething problems as considered below.

3.7.3   Dependencies on the project

The main dependency is the disruption and delay caused by software teething problems; hardware problems are normally very infrequent unless some new product is being used. The software faults are caused by residual design and coding defects, and the number increases with the size of the software. As described in the following chapters, even if there is a good standard of quality control, there are likely to be between about one and four residual defects per thousand lines of code after final testing. Thus, a system with 100,000 instructions may still have a few hundred defects when the operational system is launched. And most of these will appear during the initial months whilst building up to the full use of the system. It is therefore important that a target level is set for the number of defects to appear within the introductory period.

These disruptions, the consequential delays, and the large amount of effort spent on testing can be minimised by effective quality control during the software development, as described in Chapter 5 of this book. Guidelines are also given in Chapters 4 and 5 on the prediction of defect levels. The forecast of defects will also help to determine the optimum phasing of the development, since enlarging the size of a system increment will increase the number of defects, and hence the number of operational teething problems.

3.7.4   How the design affects the reliability of the system

The system can be specially designed to reduce the impact of operational breakdowns, although this will be expensive. For example, the hardware can be enlarged to increase the resilience of the system so that a spare unit can be automatically switched into service when a failure occurs; but this only affects the infrequent hardware breakdowns and does not provide a safeguard for software failures.

Fortunately, many system breakdowns caused by software only occur in rare combinations of operational circumstances, and such failures may be by-passed when the system is re-started — after gathering evidence of the fault. In such cases, the duration of the service interruption depends on the system recovery time (the time needed to restore the system to normal operation), and this may be reduced to some extent by special construction of the design. The software can also be specially designed to improve reliability by restricting the impact of some failures to the one affected application or sub-system, thus avoiding any disruption to the overall system and to the other concurrent live applications.

3.7.5   The workload plan

From the loading plan, as indicated in Figure 3.8, and from the prediction of defect levels, it should be possible to forecast reliability targets, such as those shown in Figure 3.9. The dashed-line graphs show how the reliability would gradually improve in an idealised, stable environment. But the realistic pattern

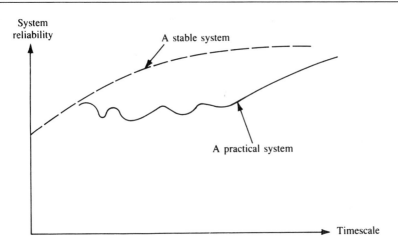

Figure 3.9
Operational reliability
profiles

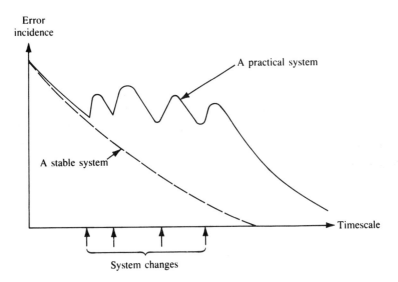

is shown by the solid-line graphs; these reflect the surge in the number of teething faults which normally occur following a change to the system or to the loading, and which delay the reliability improvement.

3.7.6 Management appraisal

Construction of such a loading projection will certainly help the two parties to form a common view of how the system may be introduced. However, whether such a view is satisfactory for the purchaser is questionable, and it may be necessary to carry out further investigations, such as those listed below, in order to arrive at an acceptable plan:

- The phasing of the development and loading of the system may need to be graduated to reduce teething problems.
- The recovery time of the system after a catastrophic failure may need to be reduced by modifying the software.
- Other design changes may be examined to improve the system resilience, and to limit the impact of failures; but remember, extra hardware is only a safeguard against hardware failures.

Once the design issues have been resolved and the project has been launched, it will not be easy to alter the software development strategy. However, the phasing of the system loading can be changed by varying the workload and the extent of connected hardware, or by delaying the introduction of a system increment. Such changes may be made dynamically during the initial use of the system in order to reflect the actual achieved reliability or business circumstances. However, remember that any change will be expensive if the overall timescale is delayed.

Conclusion

Much of this chapter, and particularly the issues in the final two sections, have indicated how management can appraise both the design and the requirements. There has also been some emphasis, in this last section, on the inter-dependence between the design and the implementation plan in assessing the introduction of the system. However, the following chapter will show how the planning task raises other issues which affect the development phasing and introduction plans; and it will also show how the planning task can be a valuable check and balance on many aspects of the design.

4 Project plans and estimates

Objectives and principles

4.1 Introduction

This chapter aims to answer the following question:

> Given the notorious difficulty of obtaining a reliable prediction of implementation cost and timescale, how can such a forecast be obtained?

The key word is 'reliable', which implies confidence in the estimate, even though it will be expressed within fairly wide limits of at least plus or minus 10 per cent. Despite the coarseness, it will be shown that such a forecast requires a substantial amount of planning work and, in most cases, there is no short cut to avoiding that effort.

It is difficult to plan the implementation of a large project, especially since there is no standard method or approach — even experienced managers have different views on what should appear in a plan at the commencement of a project. However, the approach described in this chapter should provide a guide for producing a sound plan; it also suggests how management can appraise the plans and estimates — to avoid being deluded with false security by an 'acceptable' estimate which does not have a sound basis.

This chapter is divided into two parts in order to distinguish the principles of the approach from the description of the actual process. Thus the first part justifies the need for a project plan as the basis for a firm estimate of the cost and timescale — this is referred to as the 'planned approach'; it also clarifies some of the underlying principles of estimating and compares the use of estimating models with the planned approach. On the other hand, the second part outlines the sequence of steps in the planning and estimating process, and gives the guidelines for the managers' appraisal.

Details of the estimating method are given in the Appendix, as a supplement to this chapter, and this is recommended reading for all computer practitioners.

It may be thought that this subject is not important for purchasers who have a fixed-price contract where the contractor is responsible for the reliability of the costing. However, all purchasers need to be confident that the contractor is well qualified to do the job, because the business will suffer if the new system is not satisfactorily completed; and there can be no absolute guarantee of success because contractual commitments only provide limited financial protection. Therefore, since evidence of project capability can be found in the plans and estimates, this chapter should be relevant for all managers who are involved with any large project.

Although it is assumed that the project may include a new hardware installation and a communication network, the most difficult planning task is for the software development and this is therefore the main subject of the chapter.

Project estimates should not be limited to the duration of the project because the purchaser needs to forecast the running cost over the life-time of the system; therefore, the proposal should provide some basis for costing the on-going operational activities, although these are outside the scope of the project. The main elements in a life-time costing are illustrated in Figure 4.1. The upper part of the graph shows the costs of the project development, the staffing and development facilities, whilst the lower part shows the costs of operation, maintenance and of the 'bought-in' system products and facilities.

Figure 4.1 Life-time cost profiles

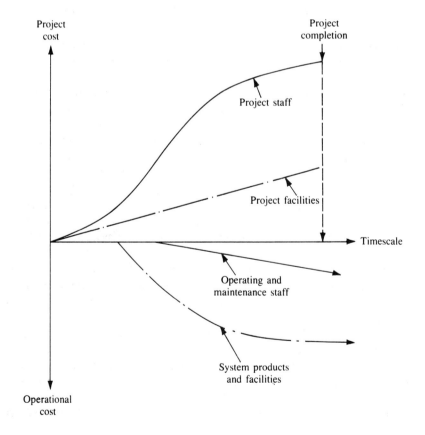

4.2 The need for sound planning

Around 20 per cent of the total staff cost may be used in the design and planning stages. The need to limit this investment often results in pressure to expedite the project decision despite the danger of a premature estimate which may not be reliable enough for a budgetary commitment, or a fixed-price bid. This dilemma has encouraged the development of estimating models, several of which are available for use relatively early in the development — even before the project is planned. However, as discussed later in the chapter, the reliability of the models is questionable, and, in the author's opinion, they should not be relied upon to produce a firm costing, except in special situations; none the less, models may be useful in providing a preliminary estimate — as an adjunct to the approach which is suggested.

In the recommended approach, the estimate is based on how the design can actually be implemented, rather than relying on a theoretical view of what might be done. The plan should be endorsed by the project manager in order to obtain a commitment and accountability — and this should also increase confidence in the estimates.

4.2.1 What is involved in planning?

The planned approach involves the following steps:

- The activities in the project task are identified and dissected down to a sufficiently low level until each can be gauged reliably.
- The resource and timescale are estimated for each activity.
- The project plan is constructed to incorporate all activities and to indicate the overall timescale and cost.

The work should be carried out by experienced practitioners, preferably the nucleus of the potential project team, and it should be closely directed by the project manager to ensure that the plan actually reflects how the project will be controlled. And, since little guidance is given in the literature about planning the final testing stages, this subject is given special attention.

An illustration of some of the problems which arise in costing a project is given below.

A contractor, tendering for a very large and pioneering project, produced a fixed-price quotation to develop the required system. Unfortunately, the project manager did not participate in the design stage and the costing was based on the system architecture and outline project plan, as produced by the senior designer. Furthermore, none of the designated senior project staff were involved in the planning or estimating since they had not yet been selected (this awaited the appointment of the project manager). However, two other senior designers did review the estimates to produce independent forecasts.

Case history 1

The bid price was based on a balanced view of the three different estimates — they were set at 50 per cent, 80 per cent and 100 per cent, relative to the highest estimate. In making a decision, account was taken of the known attitudes and track records of the estimators; one was known to be very cautious, whilst another was known to be optimistic. Eventually, the decision was made to bid at 70 per cent of the highest estimate.

The contract was won since the bid was lower than those of the competitors, and the project manager was then rapidly appointed, followed by the nucleus of senior staff. But, after the staff evaluated the design, they found that it had insufficient depth, and that the plan was impractical and too sketchy; it was therefore necessary to spend about four months on re-design and planning to produce a sound basis and costing for the project.

The eventual costing was about one third higher than had been quoted, and the timescale required an extra six months, in addition to the four months already spent on the re-design and new plan; part of the extra schedule was needed to phase the introduction of the system instead of relying on a 'big bang' approach.

The following lessons arise from this experience:

- The people who produced the estimates were not accountable because they were not responsible for the project.
- As the estimators were designers, rather than managers, they were not qualified to appreciate some of the practical difficulties which face project managers, for example in recruitment and in introducing the system.
- The design was not checked thoroughly, as was suggested in the preceding chapter; yet this is particularly important if some designers are not to be members of the project.
- The project plan did not identify the tasks in sufficient detail to indicate how the project could be accomplished.

We will consider how to avoid the problems listed above in the following sections but, first, we need to clarify the scope of a project proposal.

4.3   The scope of the project proposal

Projects are normally authorised after a proposal has been submitted which states how the design can be implemented at an acceptable cost. Such a proposal is assumed to include the following:

- an implementation plan of all project activity;
- a costing of the staff and other resources;

• arrangements for the on-going care of the system;
• procedures for controlling progress of the project and for meeting the commercial and contractual constraints.

Although the bulk of this chapter is concerned with the first two items, the maintenance aspects are also described in this section, and an indication of the more formal procedures for controlling the project is given at the end of the chapter.

4.3.1 *The fringe activities*

In addition to the development of the computer system, there are some related activities which may be outside the scope of the project; these are mainly user-orientated tasks, usually carried out by the purchaser's staff, in parallel with the development of the computer system. The tasks include training the end-users, generating the input data, and the preparations for distributing the results within the business. This work, together with plans for the operation and maintenance of the system, should be synchronised with the project plan; but it should be controlled by the purchaser's operational authority (see Section 2.6).

Although the beginning of a project is well defined, the end depends on the acceptance criteria for the project, and on how it is to be introduced into operational service and maintained. This final stage is considered further, after giving an outline of the implementation plan.

4.3.2 *The implementation plan — an overview*

Although the emphasis is on the software development, a similar approach applies in the development of any special hardware. The plan extends from an approved design architecture up to the final acceptance tests, which should also include some operational proving of the system. A phased approach is usually adopted for very large systems, where the development is organised in successive increments to make the implementation and introduction more practicable.

When the project plan has been expanded sufficiently for reliable estimating, the tasks in the plan are termed 'activities'; hence the plan is regarded as an 'Activity Plan', which has two main sections:

1. The productive activities, leading up to the final testing and acceptance of the developed system; these plans are the main subject of this chapter.
2. The supporting activities, which provide the ancillary deliverables and some supporting facilities for the main-stream development; these are easier to predict than the productive tasks, and are only briefly described in the chapter.

The number of project staff varies during the project, as is shown for the single-phased project in Figure 4.2; the peak level occurs during the coding stage, as indicated by the timescales of the project stages in the lower part of the graph. The end of the project is shown as varying from project to project, and this is elaborated upon below.

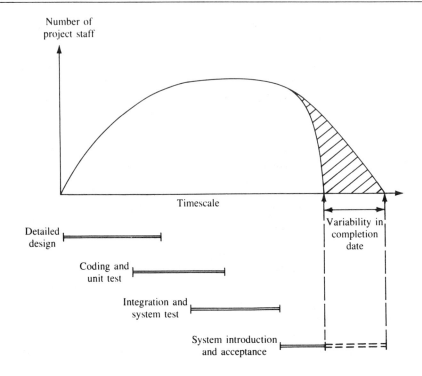

Figure 4.2 Project
staffing profile

4.3.3 Project acceptance

Although there is usually some form of acceptance test before the system is
introduced into live operation, some criteria usually remain to be tested under
live running. This applies particularly to the performance, reliability and capacity
tests, which involve exposing the system to the actual workload for a prolonged
period. However, some of these tests may have to be simulated because they are
difficult to apply, for example the peak loading only occurs at infrequent intervals,
such as the year end.

It is also not easy to specify how to verify some criteria in an objective manner
— particularly reliability — and the difficulty has sometimes been 'avoided' by
vague and subjective statements such as 'demonstration of satisfactory running';
but this is a recipe for disputes because the project has no measurable target.
It may also allow some customers, particularly the more powerful ones, to impose
a subjective viewpoint. For example, in one particular case, the director of a large
business organisation defined his version of acceptance criteria — he stated that
reliability would be satisfactory if the 'flag was up', whereas the contractor had
failed if 'the flag was down'!

This example illustrates the dangers facing a project manager in negotiating
acceptance criteria for reliability and performance. But, although the criteria should
reflect the real business needs, especially the quality of service to customers, they

should not go beyond the defined requirements. Some examples of objective measures are given below:

1. Quality of the software. Unresolved and outstanding software defects should not exceed a given total, as expressed by sub-totals for defined priority categories; and these residual defects should be resolved within a stated timescale. (Any subsequent defects should be covered by a warranty for the first year or so of operation.)
2. Reliability. The serviceability of the system should exceed defined levels over both short and long periods of time (as described in Section 3.4).
3. Performance. The performance of the system should exceed well-defined levels; for example, the response times for particular applications at user terminals should be less than a specified number of seconds for a given load (also described in Section 3.4).

In planning the introduction of the system, the aim should be to balance the growth of the user workload with the evolving capability of the system (see Section 3.7). However, it is difficult to control progress in this final stage because of the unscheduled delays which often arise. These may be attributable to either the purchaser or the project authority; for example, teething problems may cause delay; or the loading of the system may be held up by belated enhancements requested by the purchaser. It is therefore necessary to schedule some contingency, which may include the use of simulated loading tests to replace real testing at full load if the build-up is much delayed; there should also be some agreed formula for compensating the 'innocent' party affected by a delay.

4.3.4   Operation and maintenance of the system

A substantial part of the life-time cost is for operating and maintaining the system, as indicated in Figure 4.1; and these services should be planned by the potential operational authority. However, the project team usually has to develop many tools for the system housekeeping and maintenance. Although these on-going activities were described briefly in the preceding chapter, some aspects of software maintenance are now considered further, because they impinge on the implementation plan. (Hardware maintenance is assumed to be provided either by the manufacturer or by a specialised maintenance contractor, and is not usually closely linked with the development activity.)

The majority of teething problems are caused by software defects, and although most should be solved before system acceptance, some residual defects will remain. These can be covered via a maintenance contract, since they will cause further faults over the system life-time. The software maintenance staff also need to have a 'total system capability', based on an understanding of the overall system and on good problem-solving skills; then, they can determine whether a 'grey' area fault is caused by hardware or software — this is very important because, when these problems occur they often cause much more trouble than the more straightforward faults.

Although software maintenance declines as the system stabilises, further faults may arise whenever changes are made to the system or to its loading; thus the amount of maintenance depends on the extent of future enhancements; and, for large systems, software improvements are often continued over several years. It is therefore sensible to combine software maintenance with future development work, and, because similar skills are required, the dual role makes it easier to provide the 'critical mass' of skills to cover the whole system. This also explains why it is more appropriate to use the term 'software support' rather than 'maintenance'.

The software support may be carried out by retaining some project staff or, if contractors have been used, a new team may be formed which overlaps with the project team during the acceptance period.

4.4   Basic characteristics of the estimate

As the relationship between the staffing level and the timescale is fairly complex, this is considered first to set the background for examining how the estimate can be expressed to take account of project risks.

4.4.1   Staffing profile

The staffing cost is indicated by the area under the graph in Figure 4.2, and, although this is influenced by several variables, considered later in the chapter (see Section 4.5), it is roughly proportional to the size of the software, as expressed by the number of program statements.

The staffing should gradually increase and decline at the beginning and end of the project, as shown in Figure 4.2. Graduating the build-up of the staff in this way is the most efficient form of resourcing, since discontinuities caused by large and rapid changes in staffing are costly and may even be impracticable (Putnam 1980); for example, there is a limit to the number of staff who can be recruited and absorbed into the team within a given timescale. Therefore, a major discontinuity in the staffing profile is a symptom of an unrealistic staffing plan.

4.4.2   Timescale

Many projects are constrained by having to meet a completion deadline, even though the project plan may show that a longer timescale is needed. Although the planned timescale may be condensed to some extent by increasing the staffing level, the reduction is limited by the extra number of staff who can be obtained and effectively deployed. And, as the timescale is reduced in this way, the staffing cost will escalate because more time has to be spent in staff communication and co-ordination. Thus, there is little, if any, gain in productive effort by increasing the staff number above a certain level; however, this does depend on the skill level of the extra staff, since specialists are obviously much more useful than unskilled people.

The suggested method for exploring the cost and feasibility of different plans is to use trial and error calculations of the staffing needed for different timescales in each stage of the project; this will then highlight the extra cost of an earlier completion. Such a pragmatic approach will also provide greater insight into the criticality of the different stages in the project, as is illustrated below.

A plan and estimate was produced for a project which was forecast to take twenty-four months to complete. However, there was a particular need to complete the project in a shorter timescale, i.e. in twenty-one months. The project manager accepted the challenge of revising the plan — he could not argue that such a comparatively small reduction, of under 20 per cent of the timescale, was impossible, especially since extra staff could be provided. The directing management also realised that there is always some elasticity in a project team, and it believed that the timescale could be further reduced by 'running a tight ship' with highly motivated staff.

However, it proved to be very difficult for the project manager to shorten the timescale for the detailed design since relatively few key staff could be deployed and additional specialists would only cause confusion and delay progress. He felt that the coding stage could be shortened — but only by two months — if 30 per cent more staff was provided. He also judged that the duration of the final testing stages could be reduced, but only by one month, by retaining the additional programming staff.

The new plan was accordingly drawn up with a twenty-one month schedule. But, since there was no apparent contingency provision, the project manager was asked to state the probability of meeting the timescale. He replied that the new target was 'achievable' but was fairly high risk and depended on having a 'fair wind and no unexpected problems'. This view did not make the directing management feel that it could confidently commit to the required timescale, and it thus had to make provision for possible delay whilst urging the manager to apply all possible effort to achieve the deadline.

Case history 2

The following lessons arise from this episode:

- It shows how the relationship between timescale and effort differs in each stage of the project.
- By expressing the risks in such a vague, subjective way, the project manager avoided some responsibility for any eventual delay, and he did not help the directing management to make a decision.
- Since there was no declared level of contingency, it was uncertain whether

the plan reflected a conservative attitude on the part of the project manager, or whether it would fully stretch the project team.

The above episode illustrates the sort of pressure which is often applied to project managers — to reconcile their staffing and timescale forecasts with commercial constraints. In this particular project, the manager should have expressed the risks in such a way that the directing management could make a sound judgement of the risks. We will now consider how this may be achieved.

4.4.3 The impact of risk on the timescale and cost of the project

Assuming that the design is viable, most implementation risks can be represented by the probability of delay and/or excess cost. Apart from excess cost for the operational system caused by extra hardware, the main impact of risk is a delayed timescale, which also causes a consequential increase in the development cost.

By assessing each hazard, an optimistic and a conservative judgement can be made of the timescale for the affected activity; then, by forming an overall view of all activity estimates, it is possible to forecast the earliest and latest completion dates for the project. The significance of the timescale limits should be described as meaningfully as possible. Thus the early date may be regarded as achievable with 'a fair wind', allowing a minimal contingency of extra resource and timescale to overcome major hazards, whilst minor hazards are assumed to be covered by 'good management'; this judgement may be quantified with, say, a 50/50 prospect of achievement. On the other hand, the later date should reflect a conservative provision for the hazards, and the judgement may be quantified with, say, a 90 or 95 per cent probability of completion before the forecast date.

If there is significant uncertainty in the resource costing for each timescale, the cost may also be expressed at two levels. The higher costing should include a conservative provision for the variable cost of such items as recruitment, hiring contracted staff, overtime payments and chargeable machine testing; this should give, say, a 90 per cent probability of containing the actual cost. On the other hand, the lower cost level should be the optimistic prediction, with, say, a 50 per cent probability of containing the cost.

Figure 4.3 indicates how the impact of risk on the estimates may be represented by two costings for each of the two timescales. The shaded area, which identifies the limits of the cost and timescale, provides the focus for the final risk assessment and for setting the project objectives — somewhere between the limits. In considering the project manager's assessment, the directing management should probe the underlying basis — the project plan, especially the more hazardous activities — to check on the manager's judgement. This helps to decide where the probable outcome will lie, between the optimistic and conservative forecasts of the project manager.

Where contractors are involved in competitive bidding, the commercial pressures to minimise costs usually dictate a sparse use of resources and a tough challenge

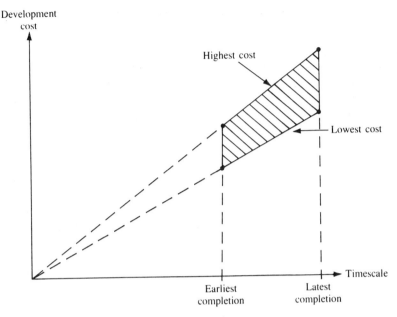

Figure 4.3 Range of estimating limits

for the project. And such a climate makes it more likely that unrealistic and optimistic assumptions will be made. In other situations, the absence of competitive pressures allows a more relaxed approach and, possibly, a lower level of project efficiency; it is then particularly important that the directors can set cost-effective objectives based on their assessment of the reliability of the estimate, and this is considered in the next section.

4.5   Estimating reliability

Any estimate depends on the experience and judgement of the people involved and it should always be checked by other experts. A comparison may also be made with an estimate produced by one of the theoretical modelling methods (subject to some precautions), and, since these methods are commonly used, they are considered briefly below.

4.5.1   Theoretical methods and estimating models

Amongst the various publications on this subject, the books by Jones 1986 and Boehm 1981 give a comprehensive view of the many variables to be taken into account when estimating a software project; these books also indicate many pitfalls and complexities in making estimates.

   The variables affecting an estimate may be considered in the following two categories:

(a)   system variables, relating to the nature of the system, for example its size, complexity and performance;

(b) project variables, which relate to the implementation of the project; they include the development method, skill levels, aids and the development environment.

An estimating model is based on a theoretical view of how the staffing and timescale can be calculated by using a formula containing selected system and project variables. The primary variable is a forecast of the size of the programs; this is usually expressed by the number of instructions although there are other more experimental methods which gauge the size by design characteristics of the input and output data and the record files. The estimating formula has usually been validated by comparison with the results of past projects.

One of the more common types of model, COCOMO (Boehm 1981), exists in three versions to provide increasing accuracy of estimating — by using more data about the system and project. An indication of the simplest version, the 'basic model' is given below, although this is probably only suitable for rough preliminary estimates.

$$\text{Staffing} = M(\text{size})^e$$

where

'size' is the forecast total of program instructions;
'M' and 'e' are given constants.

(Another equation is given to express the inter-relationship between the timescale and the staffing.)

The scheduled timescale varies much less than the effort with the size of the system; this is because business pressures force most large projects to be completed within, say, eighteen months to three years.

In the more detailed COCOMO models, the fixed multipliers in the basic version are modified by the composite evaluation of many other variables; these relate to the nature of the system, the project skills and the development environment. And, in the most detailed model, the variables are assessed separately for the different stages of the project and for different levels of system component.

4.5.2   Limitations of estimating models

Apart from the difficulty of selecting a model from the several available products, there are two common limitations.

Firstly, although the input data to a model aims to represent both the system and the project environment, it does not fully reflect how the project is to be carried out, nor can it do so unless the judgements are made by the accountable manager; for example, models cannot usually allow for project strategies such as phased development.

Secondly, the theoretical nature of the method means that a rather blind trust has to be placed in the validity of the model unless there is some prior experience.

Models are therefore more likely to be reliable if they are used for successive projects in known environments where records are kept about past projects and where the management policies and development facilities are reasonably stable; the model may then be specially calibrated to reflect a known track record. However, such conditions do not apply to many large projects because the development strategy and environment are tailor-made, and the project staff come from different backgrounds.

Some other limitations are given below:

- The impact on an estimate of changing the staffing level or timescale varies substantially for different models (this may not be widely appreciated). For example, in the extreme case, one model predicts that less effort is required if the project timescale is extended, whilst other models predict that more effort is required. The author's view is that such variations should be assessed by considering the practical implications on each stage in the project plan, as was shown in the preceding case history.
- Care is needed in interpreting claims about the historical validation of models: validating the formula does not guarantee the reliability of a future estimate by such a model. For example, in 'validating' a model by comparison with past projects, the known actual values of the variables may be applied to the model, especially of the most important variable — the size of the software. However, when making an estimate, the variables have to be judged 'before the event' and these are difficult judgements which will affect the resulting estimate considerably.
- If the model is used to provide an estimate for a firm timescale and costing, the subsequent project plan may be constrained to conform to the estimate. 'Putting the cart before the horse' in this way may result in superficial planning which does not expose an unsound estimate — until it is too late when the project is being implemented. Alternatively, if the project is well planned subsequent to the estimate, it may then be revealed that the model view is optimistic, thus posing a serious dilemma: either to revise the estimate to make the task viable, or to attempt to achieve an over-ambitious plan; but in the latter case, it may soon become apparent to both customer and project staff that the project is not on a sound course.

Such caveats make it advisable to obtain expert advice about using a model for the first time. Additional information about the reliability of certain models may be obtained from the references (Kemerer 1987, and Kitchenham and Taylor 1984).

4.5.3 Some benefits of estimating models

Although an estimating model may not be relied upon for a firm estimate, the following benefits indicate how a suitable model can be potentially useful as an adjunct to the planned method:

- The many variables affecting the estimate, which are incorporated in models, provide a useful check list of distilled experience of many past projects.
- Where a model has been well tuned to reflect the achievement of past projects, the estimate is a useful check on the bottom-up approach in the 'planned method', especially for any under-estimate of the overheads and unproductive time.
- Comparison with a model may guard against an over-generous allowance of time or money when the estimate is not constrained by commercial pressures or subject to a second opinion; remember that Parkinson's Law will usually apply to ensure that the resources fill up the available timescale.

A more detailed appreciation and assessment of modelling methods may be obtained from Boehm (1984), Macro and Buxton (1987) and from Londeix (1987).

4.5.4 *Justification of the planned approach*

This approach, based on an activity plan and on the commitment of the project manager, has the following advantages:

(i) *More reliable assessment of the task*

Because the software is dissected into small and well-defined constituent activities, the size can be gauged more accurately. A detailed view of a group of inter-dependent activities from part of a project plan is shown in Figure 4.4 which indicates how such an activity plan provides the basis for estimating, and how the staffing estimate is calculated by accumulating the effort in each concurrent activity.

Such a detailed breakdown of the task also provides other benefits as follows:

- The plan for the detailed design can reflect the actual depth of the design architecture, and also the skills of the staff to be assigned to the work.
- The impact on the timescale of staffing variations can be examined pragmatically, as in the preceding case history; the dependence on the critical paths is also illustrated in Figure 4.4, which shows how the duration of just two 'critical' activities, A3 and A4, determines the overall timescale.
- The estimate can match the chosen implementation strategy, for example by reflecting the planned overlap between stages, or by an incremental or phased approach.

(ii) *Account is taken of the quality of the implementation*

The effort spent on re-work, for all checks and tests and correction of defects, is a large but uncertain proportion of the productive staffing effort. Several

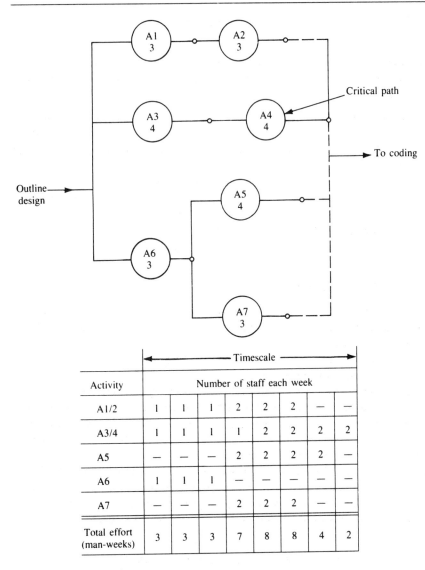

Figure 4.4 How an activity plan provides the basis for the estimate

Activity	Number of staff each week							
A1/2	1	1	1	2	2	2	—	—
A3/4	1	1	1	1	2	2	2	2
A5	—	—	—	2	2	2	2	—
A6	1	1	1	—	—	—	—	—
A7	—	—	—	2	2	2	—	—
Total effort (man-weeks)	3	3	3	7	8	8	4	2

Key: A_n / w w — duration of activity in weeks

authorities agree that it is about 50 per cent; and it reaches its highest level during system testing where the effort and timescale depend largely on the amount of error correction. The proposed method recognises this influence, especially in the integration and system testing stages where error correction is so dominant. The impact of re-work can also be reflected in the estimates of the earlier stages by making a specific provision for quality checks — and such early checks have been proven to be the least expensive method of correcting defects (Boehm 1981, and Kitchenham 1987).

(iii) Account is taken of other dependencies on management policy and capability

Many project variables, such as skill levels, are controlled personally by the project manager, whose actions and judgement affect the actual cost and timescale, as indicated below:

- Recruitment, especially for key positions, may be particularly difficult; and any late appointment for the detailed design can delay the overall timescale.
- The plan of the run-down of the project staff at the end of the project should ensure that sufficient skills are retained for correcting errors in the final stages; this crucially affects the system test, since error correction may be much prolonged if some of the people who produced the code are unavailable.
- The effectiveness of any project depends largely on leadership; for example, well-motivated staff spend less time on non-project-related activities, and these can consume up to about one-third of the project effort.

4.5.5 Conclusion

Although estimating models have improved our understanding of the behaviour of computer projects, they do not fully take account of the important practical aspects described above.

As a crude analogy, modelling methods may be compared with an architect's prediction of how much it will cost to build a house — in advance of the builder's estimate. Although the architect can assess thoroughly how the design may or should be built, the missing elements are the practical experience and judgement of the person who is actually going to do the work, and who alone can decide how it will be tackled and how much it is likely to cost. Similarly, if an estimate is produced by someone other than the project manager, the judgement of the estimator sets the objectives for the project and yet the judgement is unlikely to be the same as that of the actual project manager. However, the more theoretical forecast is often useful in providing a preliminary ball-park for the purchaser, and it can also be a useful cross-check on the planned estimate.

4.5.6 Summary of the planned approach

This is now summarised in the following five points to reflect the issues above.

1. Estimating should only be carried out by people who:
   - have the experience to foresee how the task can be done;
   - have the ability to gauge the resource and skill levels to achieve the task;
   - are accountable for their judgements; the acid test is whether the estimator will be responsible for the task.
2. The activities are organised into a network form of plan which shows the inter-dependence of different activities and the critical paths in the plan.

3. The work is dissected into small activities which allow the staffing and skill level to be identified reliably.
4. The effort and timescale are estimated for each activity and these are then aggregated to form the overall forecast.
5. The risks are assessed and allowed for within a range of estimates which reflect the high and low limits of the planned timescale and cost.

The planning process

The planning process is considered in two parts: firstly, determining the strategy or course to be followed by the project; and secondly, outlining the approach to produce the detailed plans and estimates of the software implementation. This is followed by a brief summary of the ancillary activities and costs, and finally by suggestions for a 'management-by-exception' appraisal of the plans and estimates.

4.6   Implementation strategy

The planning process is based on the architectural design, but where the project manager has not been a party to the design, it is important that this is reviewed in case there are omissions or unsound judgements, as occurred in the following case history.

A contractor was bidding for a major extension to an existing and large real-time system, comprising a network of distributed sub-systems. The design and estimates were directed by a senior consultant to match the stated requirements of the purchaser. After examining the design proposal, the purchaser accepted the fixed-price quotation.

Case history 3

The project manager was not appointed until a later date and when he reviewed the proposal he found a major design weakness caused by the incorrect interpretation of a requirement; this assumed that the processing of a major part of the message traffic would be carried out in the central system instead of in the satellite systems.

The solution to the problem required a substantial change to the design, which doubled the size of the satellite systems. The cost of the extra equipment had to be borne by the contractor, and the solution might have been much more costly had the purchaser not agreed to relax the requirement to limit the extent of the necessary re-design.

The lessons from this episode are as follows:

- The design should have been more thoroughly checked before being submitted.
- Reliance cannot be placed on the purchaser's staff to check the design — it is the contractor's responsibility.
- It is essential that the project manager has sufficient technical ability to be able to judge the soundness of crucial aspects of the design, even if this depends largely on inputs from others.

4.6.1   Re-assessment of the design

Although the review should be comprehensive, there should be some emphasis on the implementation and operation of the system because these aspects are likely to be better judged by the project manager than by the designers.

Particular subjects for review are as follows:

- the completeness and practicality of the design solutions to meet the functional requirements;
- the sizing of the system, particularly the assumptions made about the run-time efficiency of the software and the storage capacity;
- the usability of the system for the end-users;
- the practicality and cost-effectiveness of the design for both implementation and its subsequent maintenance.

A more detailed list of suggested checks is given in Schedule 1 at the end of the chapter.

4.6.2   Forming the strategy

In order to assess possible strategies, the manager should have a rough 'ball-park' view of the project timescale and staffing level. This can be formed by experienced judgement, by comparing the size and difficulty of the system with similar projects and then gauging the overall production rate with a 'rule of thumb' yardstick or one of the simpler estimating models, as indicated in Section 4.5.

Some issues to be considered in forming the strategy are as follows:

(i) Design hazards

The main risks should be apparent at this time, for example, there may be some technical problems in using pioneering technology or novel products. Many risks can be reduced by phasing the development to make more time available for solving the problems. And, although the degree of phasing may be constrained by the need for an early completion date, if the more urgent deliverables are included in the first increment, they can be available earlier than in a non-phased approach.

(ii) Timescale constraint

If there is a crucial deadline which requires a very tight timescale, high skill levels should be used for the most important tasks, such as the time-critical routines, complex control programs and any novel system concepts; greater care should therefore be taken in selecting those staff, including the project manager, as suggested in the guidelines given in Chapter 6.

(iii) Some other constraints

- Staff procurement. How quickly can qualified key staff be obtained, and will there be major difficulties in obtaining the other staff?
- Staff retention. In a long project timescale — more than two years — allowance has to be made for staff replacements.
- System introduction. Is there a plan for the transition from an existing system to the new system, bearing in mind how the business can cope with the change?
- Structure of the design. Does this restrict the partitioning of the design into implementable sub-systems to achieve the required degree of phasing?
- Implementation efficiency. Can this be improved by using aids or standard software packages, or 'macro' or 'quick-build' languages? If novel productivity aids are proposed, the claimed benefits should be examined carefully; for example, is account taken of teething problems and the learning curve where the project team is unfamiliar with the technique?

4.7   Work organisation

Although the main emphasis in this chapter is on the software development, other plans and estimates are also required for the ancillary products and supporting tasks. For a large project, this complexity makes it advisable to follow an organised and systematic approach, based on a well-defined structure of all work to be carried out. Such a logical organisation of the project tasks is commonly known as the 'work breakdown structure or WBS'; this also provides a useful framework for the activity plans and a cross-check of the completeness of these plans. These two dimensions of the planning structure — the 'WBS' and the 'activity' — are described further below.

4.7.1   The activity

This term defines that level of task in the plan which can be reliably estimated; furthermore, the completion of an activity is the smallest measurable milestone of progress, and there should be a visible deliverable — even if it is only a document. Figure 4.4 shows how the activities for the detailed design of several program modules may appear in a plan. However, it is also necessary to define clearly all of the work to be carried out in each activity, and this may be achieved by specifying the tasks in a 'work package'.

4.7.2 The work package

The work for one or more related activities, together with their associated resources, is defined by a 'work package'; for example, one package may cover the detailed design activities in the system component shown in Figure 4.4. By defining all project resources in this way, the work packages can account for all the project staffing and the corresponding budget; this makes the work package a useful aid in controlling the project expenditure (Boehm 1981).

4.7.3 The work breakdown structure

The complete set of work packages constitutes the work breakdown structure. Some possible headings for the groups of packages are given below, and more detailed sub-headings are given in Schedule 2 at the end of the chapter:

* programming: the detailed design and coding;
* system activities: including system and acceptance testing and the introduction of the system;
* other deliverables: hardware, manuals and training;
* project support: development facilities, tools and standards, and project administration and management.

An outline of a work breakdown structure (WBS) is shown in Figure 4.5, with sufficient detail to indicate how work packages may be allocated to the programming stage.

It should be noted that, whereas the WBS should specify all resources, the staffing in activity plans only covers those tasks which create some specific product; thus, whilst there may be an activity plan for producing the quality control standards and guidelines, such plans would not exist for the on-going work carried out by the quality controllers and the administrative staff. It is therefore only the 'constructive' part of the WBS which matches the activity plans; this covers the software development, the production of any related product, and the need to produce or generate any facilities and resources required by the project.

4.8   The software implementation plan

In the plan, the tasks are decomposed until the resources and timescale of each activity can be estimated reliably. A detailed method for planning and estimating is given in the Appendix, but the following outline of the main steps should be sufficient to appreciate the management guidelines, given later in Section 4.12, for appraisal of the plans and estimates.

4.8.1 Preliminaries

Creating the project plan for a large system is such a substantial task that it should be well prepared by producing a schedule of the work, and obtaining approval

Figure 4.5 Part of a work breakdown structure

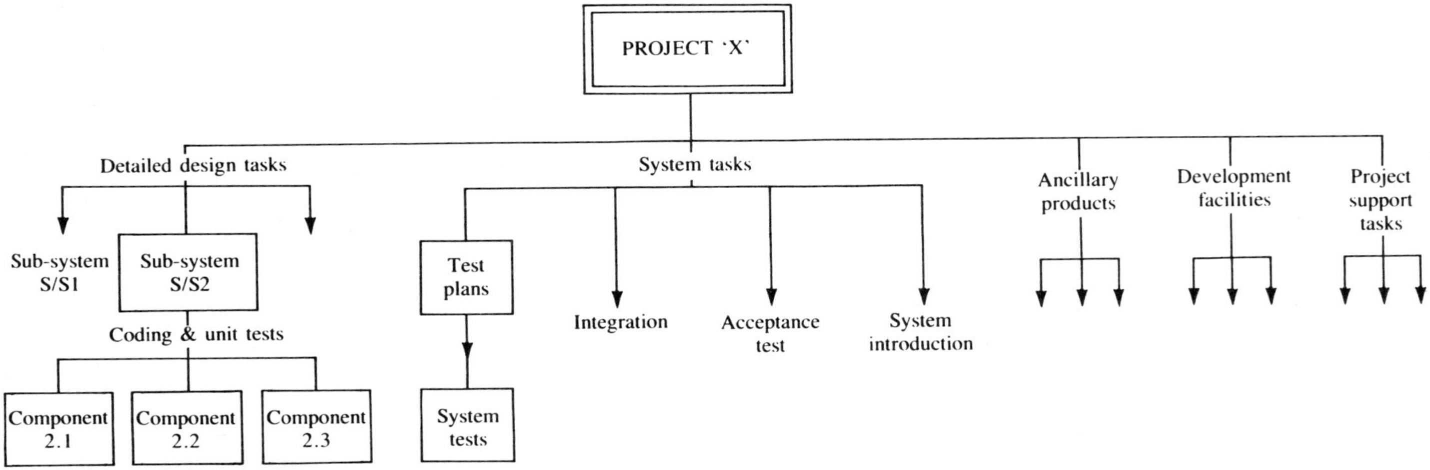

for the required resources. If at all possible, the senior staff designated for the project should participate in the planning work. However, if any of these key staff are not available, there should still be accountability for the plan, even if it largely rests on the project manager; this implies that the manager should have sufficient technical knowledge to direct the planning, although others may perform the detailed work.

4.8.2 Outline planning

Some issues to be considered in producing the framework of the plan are as follows:

1. Phasing. An incremental strategy has a large influence on the structure and timescale of the plan. This is illustrated in Figure 4.6 which demonstrates how the implementation may be phased and how risks are reduced; for example, the initial sub-system or increment may contain the less difficult developments, the second increment has the more hazardous items, and the final increment contains the remaining and low priority requirements, plus changes to the earlier increments.

Figure 4.6
Incremental
development

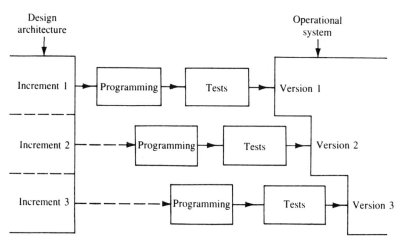

2. Terminating the project. The target needs to be well defined in terms of the acceptance criteria and the degree of loading of the operational system. As discussed in Section 4.3, this depends on having agreed plans for the live introduction and loading and for carrying out any residual acceptance tests under live conditions.
3. Major problems and risks. The approach for tackling the major difficulties should be determined. Examples are:
   - the need to examine alternative designs for any pioneering software;
   - arranging special tests for a pioneering hardware unit;
   - the need for a temporary test bed for the initial testing of the software.
4. Organisation of the development stages. This may be roughly outlined

similarly to that shown in Figure 4.7, in order to explore how the detailed design can be organised; this will help to form the approach to the coding and its subsequent integration, including the overlapping of these stages.

5. Staffing. Any procurement dependencies should be highlighted so that difficulties in external recruitment can be backed up by contingencies for the hire of contract staff.

6. Other resources. A check should be made that sufficient hardware test facilities will be available at the appropriate time.

4.8.3 Detailed design plan

Figure 4.7 re-emphasises how critical paths affect the completion timescale of the project. The dashed lines in the diagram represent the 'float' in the plan — the elapsed time between the completion of one activity and the commencement of the succeeding one. The detailed design of component 2 is shown as being a critical path, unlike those for components 1 and 3, where there is some float or waiting time.

Although the extent of the detailed design task depends on the (variable) depth

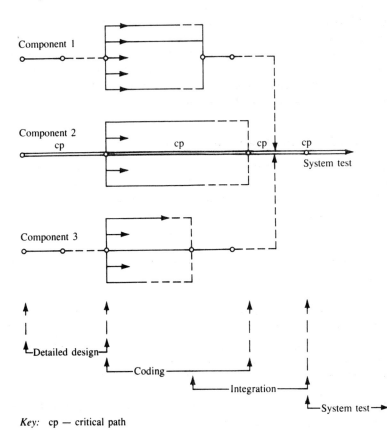

Figure 4.7 The impact of critical paths on the overall plan

Key: cp — critical path

of the architectural design, the end of the stage should be well defined by the completion of the detailed module specifications, each of which should represent no more than a few hundred coded instructions. As comparatively few staff are involved in this stage, the plan may be produced by the actual staff to be used; then the estimates can be based on the question 'how long will it take you to complete this task?'.

4.8.4 Coding plan

The coding stage is easier to plan and control, and it is also less likely to slip behind schedule. For a large project, coding only uses about one-third of the total staffing effort, and an even smaller proportion of the total timescale. It is therefore not the dominant part of the project which is sometimes assumed; and improvements to coding productivity, such as the use of macro techniques, do not substantially reduce the overall cost and timescale.

Coding is also more mechanistic than other parts of the project because it is closely prescribed by the module specifications. This implies that the estimate can be based on productivity yardsticks, although the coding rate has to be selected from a wide range; for most programs, this probably lies somewhere between a few hundred and several hundred source instructions per man-month, depending on the difficulty of the program and the capability of the programmers. Because the coders are not usually identified at this time, average skill levels have to be assumed, and whilst this means that some activities progress faster or more slowly than planned, management should be able to balance the variations to keep overall progress in line with the plan.

4.8.5 Integration and system test plan

This stage reverses the decomposition in the programming stage by progressively knitting together the tested modules until they form an integrated system. This usually involves a series of incremental builds, some of which may overlap the coding, as shown in Figure 4.7. However, the final increment, which completes the building process, will always be a critical path.

Past experience shows that the timescale for integration and system testing is often under-estimated because more software defects emerge than were anticipated. And the bulk of the problems has to be fixed before the overall system can be successfully demonstrated at the end of the test. Such a visible verification of the quality of the system contrasts with the completion of unit testing, which does not certify the standard of software quality because of the uncertain stringency of the tests; this explains why delays are much less common in completing the unit test than in system testing. And, unfortunately, the latter delay is often unexpected because the preceding stages can be 'completed' on schedule, even if the software quality is not good.

The timescale of the final tests is affected by several variables: the design structure; the concurrency and depth of the testing; and the overlap of integration with coding. But, above all, the timescale depends on the correction of defects, including access to the programmers, some of whom may have left the project.

The domination of defects in the system test makes planning particularly difficult, and, since there is little published guidance on this subject, it is not surprising that many estimates are not based on any plan. Instead, a rough ball-park yardstick is often produced — usually some proportion of the estimated effort and timescale for the programming stage. Yet, without a plan, how can there be confidence that the estimators understand the task to be performed? Even an attempt to produce a plan implies that there has been some assessment of the test activities, and a thorough approach should be able to forecast the defects and their correction, as is described in the Appendix. Because software quality has a major impact on the project, it is examined further below.

4.9   Software defects

Software defects are caused by human errors in every stage of the development, but the more serious defects are caused by design deficiencies. The extent of the problem is illustrated by the amount of effort spent on defect correction or 're-work'; this may be about one-third of the detailed design effort, one-half of the coding effort and two-thirds of the integration and system test. The amount of corrective work in the final testing stages may be even higher if there is poor quality control in the preceding stages, and this is why thorough checks of the design and code should be carried out (Kitchenham 1987).

Although there are few references which help to gauge the impact of defects, some numerical indications are given in Chapter 5 and in the Appendix. These metrics have to be interpreted cautiously because there is no standard definition of what constitutes a defect, and the source data varies widely for individual projects; however, there is probably sufficient data to justify the use of some rough yardsticks; for example, it is suggested that between two and six defects per thousand lines of program code (known as KLOC) will emerge during system testing. Such metrics also illustrate, vividly, the large scale of the correcting task — for a system with 100,000 lines of code, 400 defects may be detected during the system test!

The total number of undetected defects after the final tests cannot be determined until long after the system becomes operational. However, most residual defects usually emerge during the initial months of live use, and these will be in some proportion to the number generated during the system test because a thorough test should filter out a substantial percentage of the total. Although the number of residual defects depends on the severity of the testing, it is suggested that they probably amount to between about 50 and 100 per cent of those found in system testing.

As shown in Figure 4.8, the total number of defects is proportional to the size of the system and it is therefore more difficult to achieve satisfactory reliability for the larger systems. For example, if a system contains 100,000 program instructions, there will be about twice as many defects as in a similar system

Figure 4.8 The impact of defects on large systems

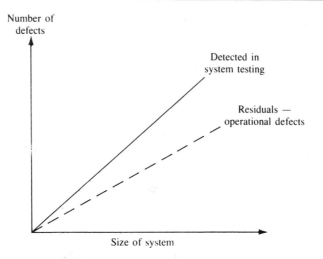

containing 50,000 instructions and any of these is a potential cause of an operational failure. The increasing scale of defects is a major reason why the development and introduction of very large systems needs to be phased in some way (although this may not be generally recognised).

Unfortunately, it is not (yet) possible to predict reliably the pattern of defects emerging prior to the system test stage. The actual number depends on many factors — the nature of the system, and the preventive quality measures taken in design and programming. These variables are explored in Chapter 5, where rough yardsticks are suggested to help in the detailed planning and control of the work. For example, 50 per cent of defects may be removed by a code inspection, compared to the removal of only about a quarter by unit testing.

In the longer term, further research and more project records will make it easier to make more reliable forecasts of defects and re-work effort. Hopefully, at some later time in the future, higher quality systems will emerge with far fewer defects and with less impact on estimating; it should then also become easier to produce reliable estimates.

4.10   The introduction of the system

After completing all system testing and pre-operational acceptance tests required by the purchaser, the introduction of the system can proceed with the following tasks:

- Preparation of the initial data files, as described in Chapter 5.
- Installation and testing of the hardware and of its control software.
- Installation of the developed software, together with tools for monitoring the performance of the system under live conditions.
- Building up the initial data load and the number of end-users of the system, as per the loading plan discussed in Section 3.7; this may include a pilot phase

for a small number of users, or there may be a parallel operation alongside existing processes until there is confidence in the reliability and usability of the system.

- Completion of the acceptance testing, including the growth of the workload to pre-planned levels.

The retention of project staff after the end of the project depends on the policy for the support and maintenance of the software. If this is not to be carried out by part of the project team, it is necessary for the new support staff to overlap the project and to gain experience in system testing and correction of teething problems.

4.11 Provision of other project facilities

Following the main emphasis on the software development, a brief summary of the other activities is given below.

4.11.1 The development environment

In addition to the accommodation and office facilities for the project staff, a computer test system is required for program and system testing; the test bed may also be used by any 'software engineering' tools which assist the development and control of the project. The test configuration should resemble the final set of hardware as much as possible, and it should have sufficient capacity to accommodate the final system tests, especially those for resilience and performance testing.

The amount of testing depends on several variables: the size and nature of the system and the number of defects. From data given by Boehm 1981, it is apparent that the number of computing hours varies widely from project to project; most of the data indicates that between about one and ten hours is used per man-month of development effort. Such a wide range is understandable because there are many variables, such as the power of the test system and the diverse nature of the various projects supplying the data. However, other yardsticks are mentioned in the Appendix to help in forecasting the extent of the system test.

The test facility may be borrowed from a part of the eventual new installation, but the equipment has to be available before unit testing begins. Although a large project needs a dedicated test bed, this can be remote from some of the project staff if communication lines are provided. After the project, a more permanent form of the test system is also required for the on-going maintenance of the software and for modifications and enhancements.

4.11.2 Provision of the hardware

The specification of the hardware configuration was discussed in Chapter 3. To avoid delays to the software development, caused by hardware teething problems, the installation plans should ensure that any novel or modified equipment is well proven before it is relied upon in the development test bed. As a further safeguard, the operational use of any novel hardware should be phased so as to spread out any residual teething problems and reduce their impact.

It is possible that hardware availability may be a critical path for the project; for example, there may be a delivery delay of a hardware extension to meet a capacity shortfall. Such risks should be covered by contingency actions in the schedule, which forecast both early and late availability dates, as for the software development.

4.11.3   Proprietary software

If software packages are used to reduce the amount of development, the specifications should be carefully matched with the detailed design of the bespoke software to achieve a correct interface; this also applies to the basic system software supplied by the hardware manufacturer.

4.11.4   Other installation work

Any major building work may delay the overall project. It should therefore be synchronised with the main development activity, and it should either be controlled or co-ordinated by the project manager. Special attention should be paid to the following potential hazards:

- If new building works are required for housing the computer system, contingencies are required for the delays which commonly occur.
- If there is a new communication network, a subsidiary plan should be produced to check that the latest timescale for its tested availability matches the project schedule.
- The accommodation and layout of the equipment should allow for any envisaged expansion of the hardware.

4.12   Management review of the plans

Management will normally examine the plans for possible reductions in cost and timescale. However, experience shows that projects nearly always run late because insufficient allowance is made for the work to be completed. Therefore, it is just as important to check that the plan is comprehensive and sound as it is to probe for possible savings; this is reflected in the following guidelines.

The suggested appraisals are categorised by the following two different dimensions of the project:

(a)   the activities: their completeness, especially of the supporting tasks, and the soundness of the estimates and the risk assessment;

(b)   the staff resources: their availability and cost, including contingency provisions.

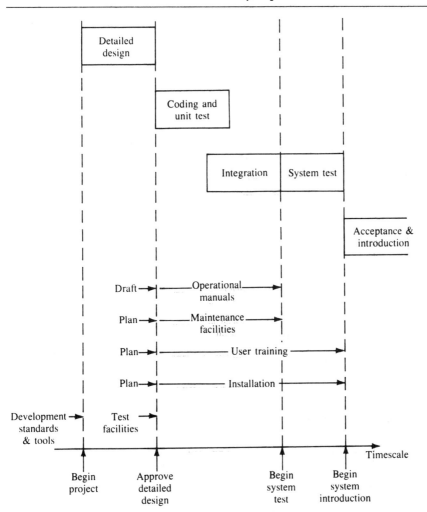

Figure 4.9 A schedule of plans and inter-dependencies

The system development and supporting activities are considered first, followed by the staffing plans.

4.12.1   The system development plans

1. Completeness. The plans should cover all activities identified in the work breakdown structure; the check can be assisted by referring to an overall outline of all plans, as shown in Figure 4.9.
2. Depth of planning. The size of activities should be sufficiently small for reliable estimating; for example, any activity taking longer than about four weeks should be suspect.
3. Quality. The activity plans should indicate that all deliverables are to be thoroughly inspected, particularly the detailed design and coding.

4. Acceptance tests. Provision for the final tests should be shown in the introduction plan, with a contingency allowance for uncertain dependencies on both parties, such as delayed loading.
5. Synchronisation of different types of project activities. There are many parallel paths in the plan where activities are inter-related. A chart, similar to that shown in Figure 4.9, should be useful in showing the main dependencies, particularly between the ancillary tasks, such as training plans and manuals, and the main-stream activities. The most important junction point is at the end of the detailed design, which should be a common baseline for all subsequent project work.
6. Estimates and risks. The main risks should be evident from the critical paths and their contingencies; these will determine the latest timescale of the activity plans.
7. Documentation. The plan should indicate that this will be available as a brief for the subsequent phase of work to be carried out; thus the detailed specifications should be completed before coding commences; and the documentation for the use and support of the system should be available to be verified during the system tests.

4.12.2   The project support plans

To ensure that supporting facilities are available in time for the main-stream development, the work required to produce project standards and facilities should be identified within work packages and activity plans:

1. Development standards. If the standards are unfamiliar to project staff, there should be a staff training plan.
2. Development tools and aids. Many of these facilities are under continuous development and, if they are either novel or unfamiliar, an allowance should be made for the learning curve and for staff training.
3. Quality control. The inspections of design and coding should follow a well-defined and disciplined process, and provision should be made for training the project staff to use the procedures; otherwise critical time will be wasted or the inspections will not be thorough.

4.12.3   Staffing plans

The following checks highlight a potential weakness of 'bottom-up' estimating, which sometimes makes insufficient allowance for staff overheads. As shown in the Appendix, these can consume more than half of the staffing effort.

1. Staff scheduling:
    *   senior staff — if any of these staff are not yet available or identified, the risk of their late arrival should be shown as a planned contingency in the 'conservative' version of the plan;
    *   staff procurement — there should be a staff recruitment plan, based on a schedule of the staff required during each month of the project;

- staff training — plans should exist if any staff need updating on any novel technology or induction of the project standards;
- termination — the plan for reducing staff towards the end of the project should demonstrate that sufficient staff will be retained to correct the teething problems.

2. Staff wastage. The number of leavers is likely to increase sharply if the project duration much exceeds one year; thus a project lasting one year may only lose 5 per cent of its staff, whereas one lasting two years may lose 15 per cent or more.

3. Absences and travel. Allowances for holidays and other staff absences should be set at some specific level, say around seven or eight weeks per year, to give an effective working time of around forty-four weeks. A special allowance for travel time should be made if project staff are dispersed at different locations, or are remote from the end-users. (It is worth noting that hired or contracted staff have a higher level of availability than permanent staff, since they are not paid for absences; this, together with the absence of salary overheads, means that the extra expense of such staff is less than is apparent from the weekly charging rate.)

4. Other overheads. A substantial amount of time is spent in various miscellaneous and unscheduled tasks connected with the project; these include reading papers and briefings, meetings, and discussions with colleagues and users about the job in hand. More time is spent in this way on larger projects because of the greater amount of co-ordination required. As this overhead effort is closely associated with the task, it may be included within the estimate of each productive activity. (A detailed analysis of this effort is given by Boehm 1981.)

There is also a further overhead for time spent in ways which are not directly connected with the project: on personal or personnel business, and on training and reading technical material. This time was estimated in one time and motion study to occupy as much as about 30 per cent of a programmer's work-day; and yet it has often been under-estimated. The overhead may be included within each activity estimate, or as an overall provision.

A method is proposed in the Appendix to allow for all such unproductive time.

4.12.4 *Summaries of estimates*

These may include a summary of the staff required in each week or month of the project for each category of work. Such a summary may also show both the optimistic and pessimistic scenarios for the timescale and costings, and an example is shown in the Appendix (Figure A8).

Organisation charts should be produced to identify the staffing at various stages of the project; these should also indicate the allocation of supervisors, say one for six programming staff, who can then be added to the staff schedules for calculating the total staffing cost.

4.13   General management and commercial issues

Much of this chapter has considered the more technical aspects of the plans and estimates. The following section gives a broader perspective of some overall managerial and commercial issues which need to be resolved before the project is authorised.

4.13.1   Control of progress and payments

Milestones should be defined for completing major parts of the project, and these can then serve as checkpoints for progress reviews by senior management.
  Some suggested milestones are as follows:

- completion of the detailed design specification;
- completion of system testing;
- completion of scheduled batches of documentation;
- completion of training of the user staff;
- scheduled delivery dates for the hardware equipment;
- completion of acceptance test prior to system introduction;
- completion of final acceptance of the system.

Where contractors are involved, these milestones may also be used for making interim payments; these are usually somewhat less than the pro-rata levels so that an amount is deferred as an incentive to achieve the final acceptance.

4.13.2   Quality control policy

The purchaser should require the following safeguards to confirm that adequate preventive provisions are being made:

1. Project standards. A documented set of quality standards should exist which specify the methodology for producing all project documentation and programs.
2. Project reviews. Arrangements should be defined for periodical reviews between contractor and purchaser.
3. Changes. The procedure for authorising changes to the baseline specifications should be defined: this should cover the impact on the timescale as well as on the cost. The practical implications are discussed in the next chapter.

4.13.3   Dependencies on both parties

Where contractors are involved, commercial safeguards for both parties should cross-refer to the technical commitments in the formal specifications of the system requirements and the project proposal. Examples of contractual provisions are as follows:

- delivery timescales and provision for variations;
- contract price and provision for variations;
- terms of payment;
- liability for damages and cancellation;
- warranties and arrangements for maintaining the system;
- rights for subsequent use of the software;
- confidentiality obligations;
- settlement of disputes;
- risks to property and staff.

Schedule 1 Check list for re-assessment of design

1. Compliance. Are the end-users involved in checking that the design fully meets the requirements specification?
2. Exceptions. Are processes defined for dealing with incorrect data, invalid operations, system overloads and hardware malfunctions? Have these processes been verified by the potential operational authority?
3. Design limits. Are there clearly defined limits for data and record storage, and for hardware and software variables such as the number of terminals and the sizes of software tables? (Overflow of such limits is a common cause of serious operational faults.)
4. Sizing. Have the projections of performance, capacity, reliability and work schedules been verified by a second party? Are the system housekeeping tasks defined and reflected in the sizing?
5. Design complexity. Does the design contain complexities which are outside the experience of the project team?
6. Design depth. Is the required expansion compatible with the skill of the available designers in the project team? Can the module specifications be produced directly from the system architecture?
7. Pioneering products. Have sufficient contingencies been allowed for the availability, performance and reliability of pioneering items?
8. Proprietary software. Is the design team sufficiently familiar with the hardware and its intimate software to be confident that the design of the bespoke software provides for all necessary interfaces?
9. Operational aspects. Are the operating staff sufficiently qualified to check the design for its operational facilities? Are the user representatives able to judge the usability of the system?
10. Hardware products. How can the capacity be extended if this becomes necessary?

Schedule 2 Outline of a work breakdown structure

A. Programming tasks

1. Detailed design for each sub-system and system component: including production of specifications of each module; data definitions and file structures; test strategies and tools; and inspection of the specifications.
2. Coding and unit testing for each set of modules: including production of test plans and test facilities; inspection of coding; and corrections and re-testing.

B. System tasks

1. Integration: including data generation; test facilities; inspection of plans; test and re-work; documentation.
2. System testing: as above plus criteria for completion.
3. Acceptance testing: as above.
4. Data generation: plans; data specifications; testing for correctness.
5. System introduction: plans; criteria for completion of the project.

C. Other deliverables

1. User manuals.
2. Operating manuals.
3. Support and maintenance manuals.
4. Hardware and communication equipment.
5. Development or modification of special hardware.
6. Proprietary software.
7. Installation environment: accommodation; power supplies and other works.
8. Training for users, operators and support staff.
9. Operational and support aids.

D. Support tasks and facilities

1. Project standards: for development tasks and for documentation; staff training.
2. Project environment: test equipment; office and other facilities.
3. Development aids and tools: staff training and introduction.
4. Quality plans: for quality assurance and configuration management; staff training.
5. Administration: for document production and record keeping.
6. Management controls: plans; progress reports; accounting; sub-contracting.

5 Implementing the project

5.1 Introduction to the management role

This chapter covers the period from the completion of the architectural design and project plan up to the live introduction and acceptance of the system, the emphasis being on subjects where the project manager can most influence the success of the project. Although the assumption is generally made in the chapter that the foundations — the design and implementation plans — are reasonably sound, some advice is also given about how to recover from an unsound basis.

The main management tasks may be summarised as follows:

- establishing the foundations for the project, particularly the staffing;
- steering the project activities to meet the system requirements and the design objectives, in particular, controlling the quality of the work and the impact of changes;
- controlling progress to meet the timescale and budget.

Although each project has its own challenges, there are two particular ones in a large project with a long timescale which deserve special attention:

(a) ensuring that the project is kept on the right course for achieving a satisfactory result despite occasional changes to the design and implementation plan — this is the main strategic challenge;

(b) at a more detailed level, giving close direction to the common cause of delay and overspend — inadequate quality.

The differing nature of these two issues illustrates why the project manager should direct matters at both strategic and detailed levels. It may seem wrong that the manager has to be involved in detail, but there is still much to be learned about the efficient development of large pioneering systems. The project manager should be able to lead from the front in solving difficult problems, and in defining the policy for some project activities, such as quality control, where there is no standard practice.

In structuring the chapter, the initial part deals with the selected major hazards — change and quality — to indicate how they influence the way in which the project is set up and controlled. Then, after considering how a project should be organised, the remainder of the chapter is divided into the following two broad

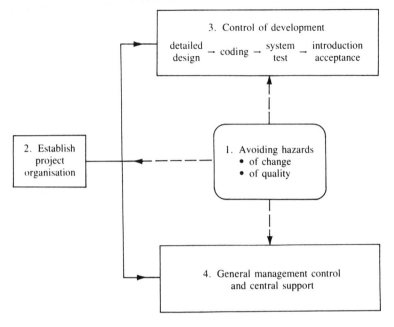

Figure 5.1 The main
management tasks
and the structure of
the chapter

subjects:

(a) how management can control progress through each successive stage of the
     development;
(b) some guidelines on the overall management of the project and on the central
     support activities.

This approach to the subject is illustrated in Figure 5.1.

5.2 Major hazard 1 — change

Some potential dangers are rather vividly illustrated in the following episode:

Case history 1	A large project was contracted out on a fixed-price basis. Prior to the award of contract, a design specification and outline plan had been submitted to comply with the purchaser's requirements, and this was 'noted' by the purchaser as apparently acceptable. The project task had been assigned to a tough and strong-minded manager who liked working to a well-defined brief, and he was then set the usual objectives, completing the project on time and within budget.

The purchaser did not appoint a full-time and dedicated manager to deal with the technical issues in liaison with the contractor; instead, the responsibility was assigned as a part-time role to the manager of the existing computer installation. This person had a rather negative attitude to the project and had reservations about both the design proposal and the capability of the project team. Consequently, there was a rather sluggish approach to the preparations for using the system, and inadequate consultation with the project manager.

Since the project manager wanted to avoid distraction from achieving the set targets, he discouraged discussion between his staff and the users. Thus, there was generally a poor rapport between the project team and both purchaser and users.

As the development progressed, some ambiguities in the requirements were interpreted by the project team without adequate consultation with the users; there were also many design improvements, some of which were incorporated, whilst others were deferred for later incorporation after agreement with the purchaser. Eventually, about nine months after the start of the project, a long list of proposed design changes was submitted to the purchaser, along with a substantial bill for those claimed as extensions to the requirements; the project manager also advised the purchaser that the changes would delay completion of the project by about six months.

The consequential dispute was not resolved because the purchaser was advised by external consultants that the system design was not practicable — it had become too complex, and fundamental modifications were needed to the user requirements to make the system satisfactory and cost-effective. The project was ultimately abandoned.

This history illustrates the following lessons:

- Both parties were too blinkered in their approach to the project; they should have been much more co-operative. For example, the contractor and purchaser should have had early discussions about preparing for live operation; these would probably have revealed some of the underlying design weaknesses which caused so many subsequent modifications.
- The project manager was not the right person for the job. A person with a broader and more flexible attitude was required to cultivate the co-operative relationship and to perceive the major weaknesses in the practicality of the system.
- A procedure for controlling changes should have been formally agreed. This would have revealed problems at a much earlier stage when there could have been a broader review of the implications. The procedure would also have prevented the unauthorised incorporation of some changes.

The specific issue to be followed up in this section is how to keep the project on a sound course despite the changes. It is to be expected that any large project of long duration will require some design modifications. This arises either through the dynamics of the purchaser's business or because of some deficiency in the baseline of the project — the requirements, the design and the plans. However, such changes should be strictly limited; they are costly and disruptive and the 'shifting sands' of continuous modifications will weaken control of the project and endanger the quality of the result.

Changes can be categorised in the following two ways, depending on whether the liability is with the purchaser or the project.

5.2.1 Changes attributable to the project authority

These are caused by a weakness or uncertainty in the design. An indication of some common problems is given below, together with possible actions.

1. Weakness in the design architecture. If a major problem arises, the project manager needs to be personally involved, since it is unlikely that anyone else has the perspective and ability to appreciate the full implications, especially the impact on the overall cost and timescale. Where the solution involves a costly and disruptive re-design, this may be eased by phasing the development so that the affected part is deferred for later implementation — assuming that this is feasible. Alternatively, it may be possible to re-negotiate the requirements to remove or lessen the problem — and this may be necessary where the re-designed system would otherwise be too complex and hazardous to implement.

2. Optimistic projection by the designers of the performance or capacity of the system. This is often discovered when the sizing is reviewed after the programming stage; for example, it may emerge that the size of the programs is much greater than had been forecast, or the terminal response times are excessive because the software is more complex than was envisaged. Possible solutions to such problems are as follows:
    *   Tuning the software by re-design and re-programming. However, management should be very sceptical about the predicted extent of the work and the forecast improvement — these are often optimistic.
    *   Increasing the size of the hardware. Although this is the brute-force approach, it is often the most reliable, easiest and cost-effective solution.

3. A specified item of software or hardware cannot be produced or is considered unsuitable. For example, a pioneering solution may be impractical or more difficult than envisaged. If there is no alternative, it may again be necessary to modify the requirement.

Because, on a fixed-price basis, such problems can cause major difficulties to contractors, they are likely to seek least-cost solutions such as those mentioned above. Thus the problem may be reduced, by modifying the requirement; or the action deferred so that it is less disruptive and less costly, by merging it with other later changes. And any acceptable solution, which minimises delay to the project, should be sought by both contractor and purchaser because this will avoid the extra cost for both parties caused by prolonging the staffing schedule.

5.2.2   Changes attributable to the purchaser

Changes to requirements are normally the responsibility of the purchaser; they should be severely curtailed, because, apart from their cost, which escalates the later the changes are made, any design modification disrupts the planned development and too much change can even de-stabilise the project. But changes are more likely to arise the longer the implementation timescale; some are caused by the dynamics of the business, but others emerge because the users increase their perception of the new system as the design evolves — then the case is made for some 'essential' new facility, improvement or correction. Such belated alertness by the users should not be discouraged altogether, as it is important to detect the need for an essential change early, rather than late. But the purchaser and users should be made well aware that changes become much more expensive the longer they are deferred.

Detecting the need for a change depends largely on the vigilance of the purchaser, users and operational authority. But the project management can and should make a contribution by periodically reviewing the requirements against the design — from a technical perspective. This may reveal some weaknesses which would not otherwise be seen, especially in the practicality of the operational system. And, although the project team is not responsible for the requirements, it will be concerned if there are major deficiencies which make the system unusable; and there is also the risk that the project may be abandoned before completion. It is therefore recommended that the project manager should be motivated in some way — even where there is a fixed-price contract — to advise on necessary changes to make the system practicable in use.

5.3   Major hazard 2 — 'quality'

Quality is an ambiguous term. In everyday use it is a somewhat abstract reference to the degree of excellence of an article; in a computer system, good quality may be regarded as compliance with all requirements, especially freedom from faults. Although poor quality may be attributable to hardware defects, it is much more likely that incorrect or unreliable operation will be caused by software faults. The high cost of software defects is not generally appreciated — even though at least half of the development resource is spent in preventing and correcting defects, even in a well-controlled project — and this cost escalates dramatically if the quality is poor. Quality control should therefore be a top priority task and should be reflected in the way in which the project is controlled.

One important lesson, which should now be generally learned, is that defects are much more expensive to correct the longer they remain undetected. For example, Kitchenham *et al.* (1986), have demonstrated that it can cost about five times as much to find errors in system test than by manual inspection of the design before coding commences, and such an inspection also improves the delivered quality of the operational system. These benefits are supported by several other authorities, including Boehm (1981), who shows how a manual check of coding is much more cost-effective than unit testing. Checks of design and code may follow one of several methods, ranging from informal reviews and structured 'walkthroughs' to the formal and rigorous inspection procedures described by Fagan (1976 and 1986); and a guideline on the use of these procedures is given in the IEE *Software Inspection Handbook* (1990).

Case history 2

During the initial stages of a project, which was on a very tight timescale, progress appeared to be fairly well on track, but problems began to appear as the system entered the integration stage. Unit testing had been completed on schedule, but after two of the three months scheduled for integration and system testing, the system was in a poor state. The main functions were still not working reliably, and there was a very large and increasing number of software faults. Some underlying weaknesses emerged during a major review of the situation when it transpired that there had not been any manual inspection of the coding, nor was there any record of the results of unit testing.

At this stage, the project manager was replaced by a more experienced and senior manager; the system test was abandoned and the unit testing was repeated until judged satisfactory. In the meantime, the system test was re-planned. Fortunately, the inherent quality of the design was sound and the system test was finally completed in twenty-one months, compared to the original twelve-month schedule. However, the final staffing cost for the contractor was almost double the budget, and the delay in introducing the system caused substantial indirect costs for the purchaser.

The following lessons arise from this episode:

- Manual inspection of the detailed design would have revealed many of the problems.
- The coding should have been inspected manually before unit testing.
- Unit testing results should be reviewed to judge the effectiveness of the tests.
- Management should have ensured that much more attention was paid to the control of software quality by all staff.

Although this is rather an extreme example, even competent managers find it difficult to control quality because they are unsure about the cost-effectiveness of preventive methods such as inspections; there are also many unproven claims about the benefits of development methodologies and other disciplines. The dilemma is made worse because there is no standard method for measuring the quality of the developing system prior to the final tests. Consequently, for most of the timescale, a project manager may be 'flying blind' unless the project is implemented in a phased manner where poor quality can be detected at the end of the first phase and be improved for the subsequent work.

To help management achieve better control, a method is suggested below for making a rough prediction and measure of software quality; this involves quantifying the defects which are generated during the development. The approach is described in some detail as it is an important part of the later guidelines for controlling each project stage.

5.3.1 *The error profile and its value in quality control*

Software defects arise mainly because designers and programmers make mistakes and misinterpret specifications; some defects are also caused by faulty corrections during the testing stages. The most vulnerable period is the design stage, when about half of the total number of defects may be generated, but most of these can, and should, be removed by planned inspections and tests, as illustrated by the error profile shown in Figure 5.2. (The terms 'defect' and 'error' are assumed to be synonymous in regard to the software.)

For a specific project, the number of errors should be roughly proportional to the size of the software code, and hence error levels can be expressed per KLOC (per thousand lines of source code, excluding comments and blanks). Apart from depending on the size of the system, the error level varies greatly for different projects, as is indicated in the survey by Musa *et al.* (1987). Despite limited published data, rough average levels have been deduced from the data given by Musa *et al.* (1987), Jones (1986), Dyer (1990), Grady and Caswell (1987) and B. Kitchenham (1987). These levels were used to construct the profile shown in Figure 5.2, indicating how errors emerge and are corrected through the various stages.

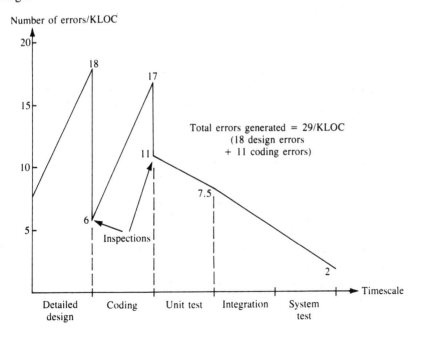

Figure 5.2 A software error profile

Although there is insufficient knowledge to predict accurately how many errors will emerge, it should be possible to produce a rough, but realistic, profile; this will also denote a careful approach to quality control, which should enhance confidence that the project will not suffer from prolonged delay in the system test because it has to compensate for poor quality in the preceding stages. And by comparing the number of actual errors with the prediction, some effective control can be applied, as is indicated below:

- Warning is given of an overall quality weakness if the accumulated number of the emerging errors much exceeds the target. This can trigger more thorough checks or other stronger preventive measures. Or it may indicate that the error prediction was optimistic and that there will be more operational teething problems than were anticipated; this may cause some re-phasing of the system introduction plan.
- It can trigger investigation into a particular component of the system whose error level is substantially above or below the average. There are several possible causes: the level of programming skill; the complexity of the system component; unclear requirements; or just carelessness.

Although there is no magic formula for producing an accurate error profile of a particular project, the yardsticks given below, if backed up by experienced judgement and insight into the underlying principles, should help to construct a useful profile. The guidelines are in two parts, reflecting the two dimensions of the profile: the errors and the correction rate.

5.3.2   The errors

The error level (errors per KLOC) or 'fault density' depends on the following:

- The inherent nature of the system. More errors are likely to arise in more complex systems and those which are subject to more change.
- The staffing skills. Errors can be minimised by higher skill, by diligent attitude and by using disciplined techniques (staff are also likely to take more care when they realise that their work will be checked by others).

These assertions are generally supported by various authorities. Takahashi and Kamayachi (1985) used data from thirty projects to find that the following factors account for most of the variation in fault density among those projects:

- The number of specification changes per 1000 lines of code increase the inherent fault density. (This highlights another aspect of the hazards of change, as described in Section 5.2.)
- A lower average skill of the programmers, measured in years of experience, increases the fault density.
- More thorough design documentation reduces fault incidence.

The survey also appears to support the assertion that development methodologies improve quality by better documentation and by effectively raising the skills level.

5.3.3 The efficiency of removing errors

An error profile can be constructed by forecasting the number of errors and the error removal efficiency (RE) throughout the development. This will also indicate the residual errors after system testing, which, as shown in Figure 5.2, are a very small proportion of those corrected.

In the example given below, the predictions of error removal assume the use of stringent inspections, similar to those advocated by Fagan (1976 and 1986). The number of errors is indicated at different points in the development; the numbers are believed to be realistic, although it is assumed that no new errors are generated after coding — whereas, in practice, some will arise, caused by faulty corrections:

After detailed design	28 errors
After inspection of design (RE = 65%)	9 errors
Errors generated in coding	15 errors
After coding	24 errors
After inspection of coding (RE = 40%)	14 errors
After unit testing (RE = 25%)	10 errors
After integration/system testing (RE = 70%)	3 errors

Thus, by predicting the RE values and the total number of errors, a profile can be constructed similar to that shown in Figure 5.2. Note that the error profile has to take account of the errors generated during coding; in the above example, the total errors are forty-three — made up of the twenty-eight up to the detailed design, plus the fifteen coding errors. The example also illustrates the greater value of an inspection, compared to the unit test. The quoted error removal efficiency for the design and code inspections is roughly in line with the measurements by Kitchenham *et al.* (1986), i.e. the combined inspections remove about 70 per cent of the forty recorded errors during the development.

5.3.4 Yardsticks of error levels

Although there are no reliable yardsticks, the limited figures available have been interpreted to produce a rough guideline; however, these should be weighted by the experience of the particular manager, and by any expected abnormally high, or low, level of quality. (Note. It is assumed that an error or defect is defined as any fault in the specifications, instruction statements or data description which, if uncorrected when the system is running, could either cause a discrepancy in the requirements or a failure of the operational system.)

(i) Overall error levels

Published figures for different projects vary widely — the higher ones, for the whole development and subsequent operation, are in the range of 50−100 errors per KLOC; other figures are much lower, down to around 20−30 per KLOC, but it is likely that these apply to projects which use high skill levels and disciplined design and programming practices. Taking account of such figures, it is suggested that the range of errors is likely to be within 20−50 per KLOC for large commercial systems where good quality control is applied.

(ii) Residual levels after system testing

Bearing in mind that most errors appear during the first year of operational running, the number of residual errors will determine the initial reliability in operation. The published figures suggest that the error level is likely to be within the range of 1.5−4 per KLOC which is roughly in line with the level quoted by Dyer (1990), assuming that good quality control is applied.

(iii) The error removal efficiency

The following levels reiterate those used previously:

Detailed design inspection   65%
Coding inspection   40%
Unit testing   25%
Integration and system testing 70%

These levels are used in Figure 5.3 in which the two curves provide a rough guideline of the upper and lower limits of error levels for most large projects. The curves show the accumulated number of errors which are detected during the course of a project; and the upper and lower curves assume a total error incidence of fifty and twenty per KLOC respectively. However, remember that this is a speculative guideline, and more research and practical records are required before reliable yardsticks can be produced.

5.4   Establishing the organisation

When the project is launched, the first priority is usually to establish the foundations — the staffing nucleus, the working environment and the project standards — so that all staff can work efficiently as soon as they join the project. These initial activities should have been specified in the Work Breakdown Structure, as described in Chapter 4, and the groundwork should have been well prepared for a rapid start to the project, especially the development standards. If the preparations are not completed before the start of the project, as may occur in competitive situations where the outcome is uncertain, there will be some initial delay, especially if the project standards have not been determined. Projects may

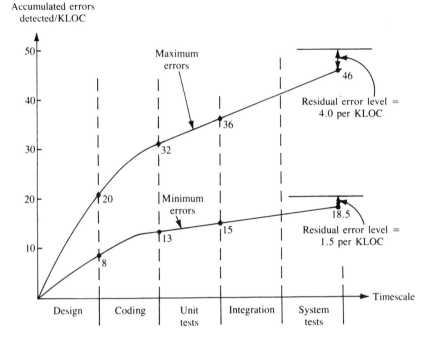

Accumulated errors
detected/KLOC

Figure 5.3 Tracking software quality

also suffer from start-up delay if the project manager is inexperienced or is appointed late.

5.4.1 Project structure

Although there is no standard form of project organisation, it is recommended that the structure for a large project should have the following main functions:

- system development;
- programming;
- quality;
- project administration.

This division of responsibilities has important advantages regarding the productive tasks, as indicated below.

The system development function is charged with ensuring that the working system does achieve the objective of complying with the requirements and design architecture. This organisational concept provides an in-built accountability for fulfilling the design proposal by making the system staff who were responsible for the design architecture also accountable for the design. By being free of the burden of the detailed constructional work, the system staff are able to concentrate on the forward planning of the final tests and the introduction of the system — tasks which are sometimes neglected when there is no such dedicated responsibility.

Programming covers the production of the software, from the design proposal up to commencement of the integration stage, when the system function takes over the remaining productive work of assembly, test and delivery of the system. Since programming is the more technical and specialised work, it may be regarded as being sub-contracted by the system function, thus allowing the programmers to concentrate, in a more narrow sense, on the quality and productivity of the programming work. This type of organisation also avoids having to rely on programmers to judge the quality of the system, although they will be much involved, in a reactive sense, in the system testing.

Such an organisational framework is illustrated in Figure 5.4. The lower part of the diagram indicates the interaction between the system and programming functions; also shown is another possible productive function, such as special hardware development, which may be regarded as sub-contracted by the system function.

5.4.2   A description of the initial management tasks

On the assumption that one manager leads each main function, the suggested set of *initial* responsibilities is given below; the on-going responsibilities are

Figure 5.4 Project organisation — and the concept of sub-contracting by the system manager

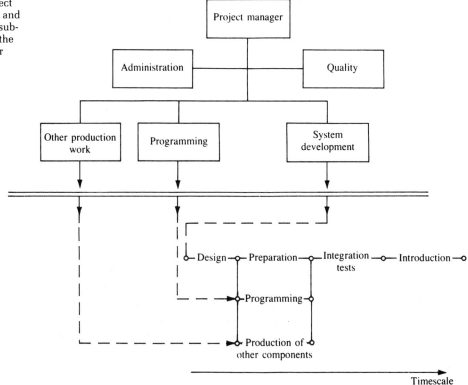

deliberately omitted from the descriptions, so that emphasis is given to the vital task of setting the project on the right track for success.

(i) System manager

- design changes, i.e. defining and agreeing the procedures and standards for changing the system design;
- planning the acceptance test, the introduction of the system and training of the users and operators;
- planning the integration and system tests and the entry of the initial data records;
- vetting the programming plans and those for any other product development, ensuring that these are synchronised with the system tasks, and participating in the formal inspections of the detailed specifications;
- planning the fulfilment of other deliverables, including the hardware, documentation, manuals and other facilities required for the use, operation and support of the operational system;
- obtaining the system staff.

(ii) Programming manager

- detailed planning, i.e. refining the project plan so that each programming activity, identified as a work package, is confirmed as practicable and controllable;
- programming policy, i.e. planning the languages, techniques, documentation, reviews, and development aids;
- handover for integration, i.e. planning the tactics for interfacing the programming work with the integration;
- staffing, i.e. planning and effecting the procurement and organisation of the programmers.

(iii) Quality manager

This person is responsible for the quality policy for the project, and defines the working practices, particularly the standards, tools and other resources which support achievement of adequate quality in the system. The manager should also prescribe or approve the inspection or review process for controlling software quality, referring to the quality targets as previously discussed.

Sometimes it is wrongly assumed that the responsibility for controlling quality lies with this manager; rather it is a duty of all project staff and the responsibility of all managers. The quality manager supports the implementation of the policy, and checks that it is being applied; this includes projecting the policy and procedures so that they are understood by all project staff, and are audited periodically. For example, the quality manager defines the form of the design and coding inspections, their scope and organisation, and how they should be reported and followed up, but the planning and direction of each specific inspection is the responsibility of the programming manager.

The main initial tasks are as follows:

- Producing a quality manual. This prescribes the mandatory procedures to be followed by the project staff. Examples are given later in the chapter (Section 5.11), and there is more detailed guidance in the IEE *Software Quality Assurance* publication (1990).
- Producing the configuration control plan. This is a special and major part of quality control to protect the accuracy and consistency of the system deliverables, including documentation, by ensuring that they reflect the impact of all changes.

(iv) Project administrator

Responsibilities include the following:

- the project environment, i.e. provision and maintenance of all facilities, including accommodation and test equipment;
- product procurement, i.e. of proprietary hardware and software for both the operational and development systems;
- documentation production i.e. the resources for co-ordinating, editing and production of manuals;
- staffing, i.e. recruitment and induction for new staff;
- budgets and accounting, i.e. establishing schedules and procedures for the recording and control of expenditure;
- controlling the contractual issues, including those related to the handling of changes to the project baseline.

5.5   Principles for controlling the implementation

Management should provide a clear brief and adequate resources for the tasks; and, if work is progressing to plan, the subordinates should carry out their work with little interference. But, from past experience, the project manager needs to be more deeply involved. The manager should ensure that the objectives for each stage are viable and are well understood by the staff; and the activity plans and staffing schedules should be sufficiently detailed for close control of progress. Then, by monitoring at the (low) activity level, any necessary corrective action can be identified in good time.

These principles are reflected in the guidelines given in the following sections for managing each successive stage of the project. The information is presented under the following two main headings:

1. A brief background and outline of the task.
2. Management challenges, where special care is needed to overcome the following hazards:
   - staffing and the provision of resources;

- planning to ensure that the course is precisely defined;
- measurement and control to review progress and quality at key milestones and at the end of the stage.

These aspects are now described in turn for each stage.

5.6 The detailed design

5.6.1 Background — the nature of the work

In this initial stage the architectural design is decomposed to provide the brief for the coders. This involves the following:

- expanding the design until the module specifications define the coding and unit testing at a sufficiently low level for assignment of the work to the coders;
- expanding the data base specification to support the coding and integration task;
- various ancillary tasks, including planning for unit testing, defining the acceptance criteria of the tested modules, and specifying the test tools and test data.

5.6.2 Management challenges

(i) Staffing

Finding and appointing the right staff is the key to success, especially since relatively few are involved in the key designer roles; and they should be filled by senior programmers who can also direct the subsequent coding work. Some of these staff should have been involved in producing the design architecture so that the initial design concepts are well understood; but, if this continuity does not exist, the original designers should be accessible so that queries can be resolved quickly.

The assignment of the staff should aim to match the task with appropriate experience and skills, especially for the more technical and specialised sub-systems.

(ii) Planning

The quality of the development work is likely to benefit by using an established design technique and methodology — preferably one which is familiar to most of the staff, although it should also be appropriate for the particular type of system. Software engineering tools may also improve the productivity and quality of the work; they should be selected well before the start of the project as well-proven devices since there are enough hazards in large projects without having to experiment with new tools.

It is important that the team leaders agree that the planned schedule is achievable; there should also be a consistency check with timings for other relevant tasks,

Figure 5.5 Expansion
of the detailed design

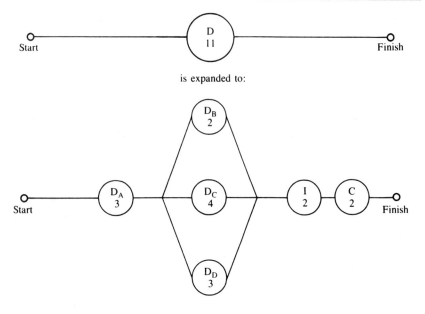

is expanded to:

Key: D — detailed design of one component (duration 11 weeks)
$D_A D_B D_C D_D$ — activities of D (duration 2–4 weeks)
I — inspection of D (duration 2 weeks)
C — correction of errors

such as user manuals and testing plans which have to be carried out concurrently and which use the common design baseline.

Figure 5.5 illustrates how the detailed design of one system component should be expanded into short-term activities lasting no more than a few weeks, so that progress can be tightly controlled. Such a plan can also confirm that adequate allowance has been made for the inspection of the completed work and the subsequent re-working; and, by defining those as separate activities, each can become a project milestone for management review. As a rough guideline to the effort involved in inspections, the production rate for a stringent inspection for detecting around two-thirds of the design errors, is likely to be between 200 and 500 equivalent lines of source code per elapsed hour — depending on the depth of the inspection, and assuming that all staff are trained in the process (Kitchenham *et al.*, 1986).

(iii) Control

The actual time taken to produce the detailed design, compared with the schedule, gives the first indication of the reliability of the overall project plan. Progress will depend much on the individual ability of the key staff, and weekly progress reviews should be held to achieve close control. Incidentally, the best way to avoid the danger of slippage is by overtime working; this can provide an extra 10–20 per cent of productive effort at low cost, whereas, if the delay is unchecked the extra cost may represent the full project team for the delayed period.

Apart from intervening if and when major problems arise, management should review the outcome of all design inspections to ensure that the project is on sound foundations before entering the coding stage. This includes comparing error levels with the target profile. Since the distribution of errors among different programs will be uneven, the exceptional levels indicate where attention is needed. For example, a high level of errors may point to an underlying weakness in the design architecture or requirements, or to inadequate skill or lack of thoroughness in relation to the difficulty of the program. And a low level of errors may arise with a simple task, a very able programmer or inadequate inspection.

5.6.3 Scope of the detailed design inspection

An indication of the aims and scope of an inspection is given below:

* checking conformance with the project baseline of the system requirements, the architectural design and the user documentation;
* checking the technical accuracy of the detailed specifications;
* updating and reviewing the sizing and performance predictions, re-assessing the predicted size of the programs and hardware, and the run-time performance;
* planning for the next stage, examining the coding and unit test plans and the estimates of the resources and timescale;
* detecting known design weaknesses, such as the limits on data volumes and record and table sizes, the interfaces with other parts of the system and the use of common modules;
* maintainability, i.e. reviewing the module structure for ease of maintenance for dealing with modifications and errors.

It is recommended that the purchaser's representative should attend the inspection, or at least a management review of the outcome, in order to gauge progress and to expedite any formal approval of the detailed design specifications.

5.7 Coding and unit testing

5.7.1 Task outline

The scope of the work is largely prescribed by the module specifications, and coding can begin after approval of the relevant parts of the detailed design. However, where components are interlinked, coding should be postponed until these components have all passed their inspections; this ensures that the coding is soundly based and avoids the need to make amendments, especially for interface changes.

5.7.2 Management challenges

(i) Staffing

Most coders should be appointed before the end of the detailed design so that they can become familiar with the specifications without delaying the project. The experience of the staff should be matched to the task, especially for the control modules and others which are time-critical or which need special skills.

(ii) Planning and control

To achieve tight control of progress, the plan should be based on small activities, equivalent to less than about two weeks' work, and there should be an adequate allowance for manual code inspections which can proceed at a rate of between about ten and fifty instructions per man-hour. An abnormal number of errors in any module can trigger an investigation: an excessive number may indicate either poor quality of programming or a task which was particularly difficult; a small number of errors may be caused by a superficial inspection, a simple task or skilled coding.

5.8 Integration testing

5.8.1 Task outline

The tested program units are progressively bound together until the complete system is ready for system testing. This process will also test some internal characteristics and interfaces between modules. However, as discussed in the Appendix, the extent of this task varies from project to project: in the depth of testing; in the size and phasing of the increments; and in the overlap with coding.

5.8.2 Management challenges

(i) Staffing

Dedicated staff should be used since this is a specialised task which needs careful preparation; the staff should also have experience of integrating similar systems.

(ii) Planning

The integration test may extend over several weeks and, for planning purposes, an activity may be regarded as a build increment and a milestone within the successive builds and tests. For tight control of progress, it is suggested that the watchword is 'build a little and test a little'. The particular method used for binding the modules together may require some test aids which have to be specially developed, such as test harnesses and data generators. The integration plan needs to be well documented because a similar process will be used for building new system versions throughout the life-time of the system, i.e. whenever there is an upgrade or new release of the software. When the plan is complete, it should be formally inspected and approved.

(iii) Control

The rate of progress depends considerably on the correction of the errors. Delay commonly arises because of referral back to the programmers to correct program documentation. This can be minimised if the integration team specifies standards for checking the documentation when the coding is inspected.

Progress can be gauged by the rate of completing each build increment, and by comparing the number of errors with the target. Progression to the next increment should only occur after sufficient clearance of outstanding errors; and delay can be tackled by assigning more effort or for correcting defects.

5.9   System testing

5.9.1   Task outline

This is usually the final test undertaken by the project team itself. Passing the test should signify that the project manager is satisfied that the development is complete, and that the system is fit for acceptance by the purchaser and for live introduction; and if the purchaser's representatives are involved, it should be possible to reach agreement on the adequacy of the test. The tests should cover all aspects of the system, both software and hardware, so that the overall system can be seen to be working and meets, at least, the bulk of the requirements. However, there are usually some limitations; for example, the data load and record files will not be at their full extent, and the complete hardware configuration may not be available. Any outstanding tests are then covered in a subsequent formal (acceptance) test and during the live introduction of the system.

The initial tests cover the basic control functions and the more common applications; subsequent tests cover all other functions and exceptions, including limit checks and error conditions; the technical requirements — the performance, capacity, reliability and resilience of the system — are usually covered in later tests. The test may be satisfactorily completed, even if a limited number of minor errors still await correction, but this depends on an agreed method of categorising errors, such as the following:

Major: errors causing malfunctions which prevent continuation of effective testing, or which would interrupt or invalidate operational use.

Intermediate: errors which cause minor malfunctions which disrupt the use of the system, but which can be avoided or tolerated in live use for a limited period of time.

Minor: errors in the documentation or ancillary parts of the system which do not adversely affect its satisfactory use.

5.9.2 *Management challenges*

(i) *Staffing*

Two teams of staff are involved: firstly, a dedicated team to carry out the tests; and, secondly, the (part-time?) efforts of the programmers to correct the errors. Because the duration of the test depends largely on the error correction, and as this is a critical path for the project, sufficient programmers should be made available — in particular to avoid waiting time for correcting major errors. The test team should also include some of the original designers so that the test plans benefit from their first-hand knowledge of the system architecture. However, some team members need to have a practical bent, with experience of system testing, so that they can follow through to provide technical support during the live introduction of the system. Some user staff should also be involved in the test, especially those who are to operate the system.

(ii) *Planning*

The tests must be designed well beforehand, especially those for technical requirements, such as resilience and performance, which may influence the extent of the test configuration. The completeness of the tests can be checked by recording those items in the requirements specification which are covered by each test increment. This may be marked up as a matrix, as shown in Figure 5.6, so that this serves as a record of the requirements to be tested.

Figure 5.6 Assurance check of completeness of the system test

Requirement specification reference	Test increment								
	1	2	3	4	5	6	7	...	N
A001			√						
A002		√							
. . .									
A112	√								
B001				√					
. . .									
B0nn									
. . .									
Nnnn									

A method for estimating the timescale of the test is described in the Appendix, and this is based on a forecast of the quality, scope and stringency of the tests.

The test schedule cannot be expanded down to individual test runs because there are too many unpredictable uncertainties; for example, the number and nature of the errors arising in particular runs, and the correcting skill of particular staff — just one difficult error can delay progress by several days! And although the plan should have enough margin to accommodate all necessary test runs, some detailed adjustments will probably be necessary in the light of progress made during the early part of the test.

The test plans should be formally inspected and examined by the programming and integration team leaders — this also ensures that they are aware of the impact on their own activities.

(iii) Control

It was suggested previously, in Figure 5.3, that between about two and six errors per KLOC will be detected, depending on the particular characteristics of the project. This means that a very large number of errors will emerge in a major system — amounting to 200−600 errors for 100 K source instructions; and the amount of work involved in testing and in making the corrections will be proportionately large. A rough illustration of the pattern of errors arising during the test is shown in Figure 5.7. (A similar illustration is also used in the Appendix for planning the tests.) The upper curves in the diagram represent the detected errors and a 'smoothed' rate of error correction. The lowest curve shows the

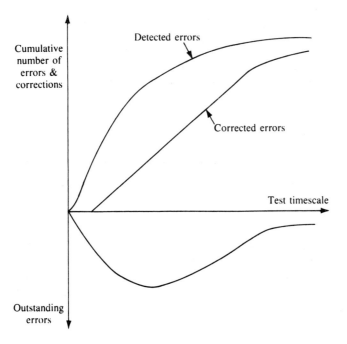

Cumulative number of errors & corrections

Detected errors

Corrected errors

Test timescale

Outstanding errors

Figure 5.7 Error profiles in system testing

difference between the upper two curves to give a rough indication of the pattern of outstanding errors during the test. (A more realistic representation would show many discontinuities — to reflect the batching of corrections, and the waiting time for applying corrections.)

Such a prediction should be useful in controlling progress, and in forecasting when the test should be completed for a particular project. For example, if many more errors arise in the early part of the test, or if correction is slower than envisaged, the task is likely to be larger than was forecast. Some control may then be applied to lessen the delay, by applying more corrective effort and overtime working; and, if this does not contain the situation, an early warning signal can be flagged to revise the completion date whilst continuing to take corrective action.

At a more practical level, care needs to be taken that critical errors from the previous increment are corrected before progressing to the next increment. Some system tests have gone out of control because the continued existence of outstanding errors has distorted the symptoms of later faults; and similar difficulties arise when faulty corrections are applied — this is why they should be carefully inspected before machine testing.

Other, more mundane, problems can delay progress, particularly lack of care in preparing for the tests; for example, incorrect hardware, or wrong versions of the programs, files and test data, or poor preparation for the test runs. Most of these problems can be avoided by good quality control, which requires meticulous and disciplined conduct of the test where everyone is well trained and rehearsed to perform prescribed tasks, and where operations are carefully recorded and checked.

5.10   Introduction and acceptance

Although the scope of this stage varies for different projects, two preliminary tasks usually have to be carried out before introducing the system to operational running: the assembly and insertion of the initial data records into the computer; and a formal acceptance test.

5.10.1   Data entry

For most projects, a set of data records has to be established within the computer before the system can be used. The records may already exist in some form on another computer system, or they may have to be assembled from other sources. In any event, the format has to be changed to match the data-base specifications for the new system.

The preparations should be reasonably straightforward, but major problems have arisen in some projects because planning was delayed until the system testing stage. It may then be found that the task is bigger than envisaged, often because the source data has not been sufficiently evaluated, and then the whole project is delayed. To avoid this danger, the data generation plan should be produced as soon as the design of the data-base is completed.

Although special programs may have to be developed to transform the data to the new formats, this task may be eased and reduced if it is possible to use the actual validation programs within the new system; this would also provide a useful live test of that part of the system.

The users, responsible for providing the data, should also be closely involved, both in the detailed planning and also in the process itself.

Special care is needed to sustain the accuracy of the data records after they have been inserted into the computer system. For example, if the records have to be updated periodically, they must be valid for the date when the system is introduced. Thus, if the live introduction fails for any reason, and the system has to be withdrawn, the assembled records would have to be 'forcibly' updated before the next version of the system was introduced.

5.10.2   Acceptance test

This is the purchaser's confidence test — that the system is fit for its live introduction. Although the test is normally specified by the purchaser's representatives, it should also be approved by the project manager as practicable and not exceeding the project commitment. If there is a really thorough system test, such a further 'acceptance' test should simply be a demonstration or confidence check; but more commonly, there will be some new tests designed by the users or the operational staff as a check and balance on the project tests. These additional tests will usually generate some new errors and, therefore, the timescale for completion should allow a few days for the corrections and re-runs. The test should also be conducted by the users and operators — to provide practical training, and to test the reference manuals and the exception procedures for dealing with operational faults.

5.10.3   Introduction and final acceptance

Ideally, the end of the project occurs when the end-users feel that the system is running satisfactorily, when it is considered 'fit for the purpose', and also when it is judged that any subsequent teething problems are unlikely to cause any major disruption. A phased introduction may include pilot runs so that the teething problems can be corrected without disrupting the business operations; the pilot runs may also be conducted in parallel with an existing system so that the new system is not relied upon until there is sufficient confidence in its reliability and performance.

As discussed in Chapters 3 and 4, the criteria for final acceptance should aim to stretch the system until it is fully loaded. However, this may take such a long time that it cannot be covered contractually, especially if the project is on a fixed-price basis; instead, the purchaser may have to rely on less stringent or simulated tests for final acceptance. However, the purchaser should have the safeguard of a warranty so that the contractor resolves any defects which arise after formal acceptance of the system.

During this stage, the project team is usually responsible for the following tasks, although the permanent support staff should also be involved:

- installation and support of the working system until the operational authority can take over the responsibility;
- correcting outstanding defects;
- demonstrating any unfulfilled requirements.

(i) The staffing challenge

The introduction task is quite different from the preceding stages because the project team has less control over the working environment. The project manager should cultivate a close rapport with the operational and user management — to agree the priorities of the work to be done, and to reach a consensus view on the state and performance of the system. This should also assist in negotiating the terms for final acceptance.

Since so much of the project work at this time is reactive in solving problems as and when they arise, the project manager has to assign resources on a day-to-day basis to match the urgency and seriousness of the operational problem. Providing support in this way may over-stretch the project team, especially if its numbers have been much depleted and if abnormal hours or shifts have to be worked. However, the operators and permanent support staff should be able to resolve some problems before calling on the project specialists; this emphasises the importance of arranging for practical training of the operational staff during the preceding stages, especially in system testing.

(ii) The planning challenge

The schedule for the final acceptance should reflect the planned build-up of the data load, and should also allow for the expected teething problems, as was illustrated in Figure 3.8. However, the loading schedule is likely to be modified during the introduction to allow for unexpected difficulties; and, as described in Section 4.3, the project should be protected against delays which depend on the purchaser, even if this involves restricting the tests or providing compensation for the prolonged retention of project staff.

(iii) The control challenge

A rough indication of the quality of the system is given by comparing the actual number of errors which emerge during the initial introductory period with a proportion of the predicted total of residual errors; however, making a sound judgement of that proportion is not easy — it has to take account of the degree of exposure to date. If the number of errors is considered excessive, extra corrective effort may be applied and the build-up of the load may be delayed.

The technical support provided by the project team needs to react promptly to operational problems. This should be well organised by drawing up a standard reporting procedure. The procedure should prescribe the actions to be taken to deal with any operational problem, and will involve both the system operators and the on-call technical support staff. The procedure should also prescribe the follow-up action to be taken after a temporary solution by-passes or alleviates a problem but which may leave some operational restrictions.

The various support tools and aids also need to be tested and used during the introduction period; and those for measuring the performance and loading of the system may be used to judge whether the acceptance criteria for system performance has been met.

5.11   Central support activity

Apart from the administrative functions, the main central task is quality control and its specialised sub-task, known as 'configuration control'.

5.11.1   Quality control

The quality manual should prescribe precautions and checks to avoid deficiencies in meeting the requirements. All tasks, both productive and supportive, which may impede the development or endanger the resulting quality of the system should be covered. The quality policy should aim to encourage and enforce a high standard of thoroughness, and to avoid mistakes. Therefore, in addition to the previously described checks and tests of the software, the quality manual should set down disciplines for achieving meticulous care in all other project activities in order to avoid defective work which delays or endangers a successful implementation. Some examples are: checks of all bought-in deliverables to detect any incorrect or faulty components; periodical checks of the maintenance of the test equipment and its environment, including the air conditioning; production of written records of all meetings in order to avoid misunderstandings and incorrect action. Examples of quality standards are given by the IEE in its *Software Quality Assurance* publication (1990), and by the US Department of Defense Standards which includes working practices to be followed by programming staff.

All project staff should be thoroughly trained in applying these procedures and, during the project, the quality controllers should check that the standards are observed.

Management challenge

In approving and implementing the quality policy, the project manager should ensure the following:

- That it is understood and accepted as sensible by the staff.
- That there is at least one independent audit of the quality control being applied by the project.

- That management set a good example: there is the danger that quality standards are disregarded when the project is in difficulty, because of pressure to solve a problem urgently. Then quality may take a back seat because management take risks in expediting the action.

Bitter experience has shown that lack of care often causes more delay in backtracking than in applying the checks; for example, a hardware fault arising from failure to check the development test bed delays the start of the next test increment; or the omission of a manual inspection of a coding amendment to solve an operational problem causes a delay of several hours because the correction fails. There is also an underlying danger because by-passing the standard procedure weakens the quality policy and encourages more such incidents. Even if such a by-pass does solve a problem, it should be followed by retrospective checks to guard against a possible, later failure caused by an undetected defect in the correction.

5.11.2 Configuration control

These controls aim to safeguard the accuracy of the development work and the integrity of the operational system against changes which arise during the project and, subsequently, during its life-time. This subject is usually separated from the other quality control activities as it is a major and specialised task which needs to be planned and controlled by dedicated staff.

During the course of a project, baselines are created from the approved specifications and blueprints of the system. These need to be kept up to date at all times, particularly when a modification is approved. Examples of such baselines are the specifications of system requirements, the architectural design, the detailed design and the hardware. To safeguard against unauthorised modification, potential changes to a baseline should be submitted formally for approval; this should include assessment of the need for the change and of its impact, cost and timescale. The configuration controllers should also have 'the teeth' to ensure that only authorised changes are applied, by controlling the safe-keeping of all baseline records within a 'secure' computer store.

An illustration of the need for such controls is when a software correction is made during system testing. Its incorporation in the system should only be authorised if there is a record that it has passed through its scheduled inspections and tests. The correction is then added to the record of all incorporated corrections. Similar controls should apply to all future hardware and software changes which are made during the life-time of the system.

Management challenge

Configuration control has received increased attention in recent years since it is very difficult to rely solely on manual efforts in applying complex disciplines and checks. Some tools to automate the controls, especially in very large projects, are sorely needed, but the control needs to be interwoven with the whole development process. Attempts are being made to produce an IPSE (an integrated project support environment) — an integrated collection of tools — to support all development activities and co-ordinate the use of the software engineering aids (Sommerville 1986). But, in the absence of a standard tool kit which is also cost-effective, it is necessary for project managers to devise their own tailored set of controls, possibly with the aid of some selected proprietary tools and methods which are available.

A further indication of the nature and extent of the required controls is given by the following examples:

- The staff in a large project work on interacting components, and a design change may require a consequential change to other parts of the system. But it is not easy to identify these dependencies and some form of reference aid is needed to supplement reliance on memory or tedious cross-reference to system specifications. Such an aid might be a computerised set of cross-references of the content of specifications to identify the consequential changes.
- Whilst the programs are being developed, detailed changes are made by programmers which do not affect the architectural baseline, but which do alter the evolving detailed design and interface specifications. These changes need to be controlled by some disciplined procedure in order to ensure that programmers record the dependencies and notify other relevant staff. Such precautions should avoid some interface errors arising during testing — where these may be difficult to detect and resolve.
- If the operational system uses a network of several hardware installations with different configurations, special care has to be taken in generating a software upgrade to match the particular site. And, where the new release has to be introduced gradually to successive sites in order to minimise teething problems, the need to link the old and new software versions may restrict some operational functions until all sites are upgraded.

5.12   Overall management controls

In addition to the technical issues described in the preceding sections, some suggestions are given about the following general management tasks:

- during the *building* period when the project resources are being established;
- in *controlling* project progress;
- in *leading* and motivating the staff.

Each of these is considered separately.

5.12.1   *Resource building*

The acquisition of qualified staff is rarely easy. Even if they exist internally, they may not be available to the project. Most important are the senior staff, whose skills should complement those of the project manager so that the collective experience is strong enough to cover the extent of the project task. These key staff should also have the project manager's full confidence — anything less is not good enough because they are not closely supervised — and their ability should be absolutely reliable. They should therefore have a proven track record and, preferably, be well known to the project manager.

The manager needs to have authority to engage staff and terminate staff appointments so that the decisions can be made promptly, and without adverse effect on the project. The recruitment of key staff is often an early test of the manager's capability, i.e. of his or her initiative, persistence and negotiating skill. Any difficulty in obtaining a key person which delays the project schedule may also test the manager's strength of character because the manager should not be rushed into appointing a person of dubious ability.

Other resources which need to be established rapidly include the accommodation, test facilities and, above all, the development standards, aids and tools for use by the project team. Since there is little time to experiment with unproven techniques, or to make a case for capital expenditure, most decisions should already have been made in the planning stage when the costs were authorised. Allowance should also have been made in the plans for any staff learning curve; and some dangers of using novel development techniques are illustrated in the following short case history.

Case history 3

A project was initiated after a commitment had been made to meet the system requirements — based on a design study and an outline proposal. One of the purchaser's requirements was that the system must be designed and documented in a prescribed methodology. But the project manager had not been involved in producing the proposal; he found that the project team was not familiar with this particular method, and that this had not been specifically allowed for when planning the project.

Unfortunately, there was much pressure on the project manager to adhere to the committed schedule; and only a small provision was made for the learning time for the design methodology, with no proper staff training. But the unfamiliarity and teething problems with the method, especially its documentation, caused the design work to slip progressively by a total of four months, and the design was completed after nine months instead of the scheduled five months.

In this instance, the manager's judgement was poor in making such a gross underestimate of the learning curve. Unfamiliar standards often cause a substantial drift of timescale and there should be an adequate allowance, even where there is a prior commitment. Otherwise, any substantial delay is likely to reduce confidence in the project team, especially when it occurs early in the project.

In this particular case, alternative methodologies should also have been considered — there may have been a case for changing the stipulated method.

5.12.2 Management control — staffing costs

The staff level is pre-set by the project plan and it is often difficult to increase the number of staff during the project because of the recruitment lead time. Hence, if the staffing matches the budgeted level, the main cost excesses, apart from overtime and other marginal costs, tend to be caused by having to retain staff over an extended timescale.

Apart from any contractual penalties and operational problems, the cost of delay can be substantial because it usually results in an extended timescale for the majority of the project staff. But, as mentioned in Section 5.6, applying extra resource by overtime working in order to avoid or minimise delay is highly cost-effective, as illustrated by the shaded area in the staffing profiles in Figure 5.8. (However, there is a limit to the amount of overtime which can be worked.)

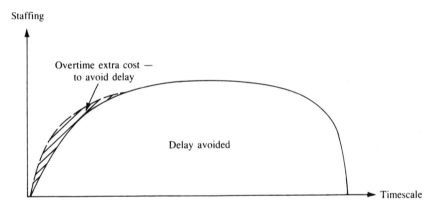

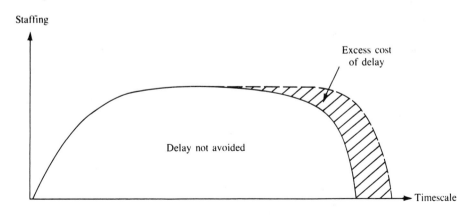

Figure 5.8 Cost control — the impact of delay

5.12.3   Management control aids

In order to reduce the complexity in managing the project resources, several techniques and tools exist to help the project manager in planning and controlling progress.

(i) Planning and monitoring techniques

The detailed project plan should be in a PERT type of format to show the critical paths and the inter-dependence between activities. Different levels of plan will be required for management and staff, and, at the highest level, a summarised plan may be presented in the form of a GANTT chart, as shown in Figure 5.9. Although this chart does not show the inter-dependencies, it does provide a useful overview of project activity. A marker can indicate the state of weekly progress for each line of activity, and also the degree of lateness or advance as related to the planned dates. Thus, in the diagram, the marker shows that at week 4 the manuals and software group A task are running one week late, whereas the group B task is one week ahead of schedule.

(ii) Management planning tools

Computerised tools exist to automate the production and updating of the PERT-type plans. These can produce different versions of the plan to reflect alternative tactics or possible impact of changes; management reports can also be generated of the resources spent to-date and of future projections. However, these tools may have to be tailored to meet the particular requirements of the project, and the project staff need to be trained, especially to ensure that they submit reliable data as input to the planning tool.

(iii) Cost control

An overview graph, as shown in Figure 5.10, compares the accumulating cost with the budget level. If this is used in conjunction with the GANTT chart, underlying trends in progress can be detected. The costs to-date can be regarded as the input resource to the project, which are compared with the project output — this is the amount of work recorded as complete on the GANTT chart in Figure 5.9. Thus, in Figure 5.10, the actual cost is shown as about 20 per cent higher than the budget level, and yet the actual work done, from Figure 5.9, is not ahead of schedule. However, the overall impact does depend on the nature of the excess cost; for example, a temporary expense, such as for overtime work, should not have an escalating effect, but the need for extra, or more expensive, staff will have a much bigger impact.

5.12.4   Management control by reviewing progress

Apart from informal discussions of specific issues, regular and formal progress

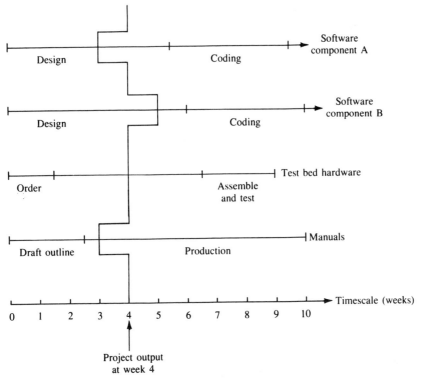

Figure 5.9 Recording progress on a GANTT chart

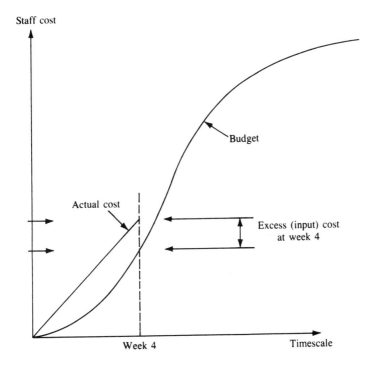

Figure 5.10 Project cost summary

meetings should be held. The formality is needed to engender a serious and disciplined attitude in those attending the reviews, and it encourages more careful preparation than might otherwise occur.

(i) Suggested aims of review meetings

- comparing progress with the planned schedule, and making the senior staff accountable for reporting any differences and for proposing corrective action;
- deciding how to tackle problems which are impeding progress, and how to prevent or minimise potential problems;
- forecasting progress, i.e. those responsible should give their prediction of progress up to the next meeting, and investigate possible obstacles which may delay the project;
- examining how costs can be kept to budget;
- resolving general problems by informal discussion of any concerns about the management conduct of the project, for example management being bogged down with details and spending insufficient time in reviewing plans.

(ii) Conduct of the meetings

Although there should be a formal approach to the meetings, a degree of informality will encourage frank views about uncertainties and current problems; to this end, the project manager should be the catalyst in arriving at solutions, rather than dictating action. However, firmness is also needed to ensure that a decision is made about every issue raised, even if it is only an exploratory action to obtain more information; also, irrelevant issues should be banned.

(iii) Defining and recording actions

All actions should be understood and accepted by the actionee. This does not always happen, and an action may not be completed because it was inadequately defined; after some days, the action may be found to be impracticable, and yet in the meantime, management has been deluded into thinking that corrective work is being carried out. Such premature and vague actions can be avoided by resisting the attempt to solve complex problems at the meeting; instead, a thorough investigation should be carried out at a side-meeting. Each action should be assigned a completion date which is followed up at or before the next meeting. The project manager should also note issues which have a wider implication — where lessons need to be applied to other parts of the project.

5.12.5 *Leadership and communication*

One of the obstacles to effective leadership and motivation of the project staff is the temporary attachment between the staff and the management — usually only for the duration of the project. It is therefore important to counter this by fostering a good team spirit; fortunately, most people react positively to a challenge, and large projects are important and prestigious. An indication of some necessary management actions is given below.

(i) Staff rapport

The project manager should obtain feedback from staff in informal chats; these can reveal weaknesses in the project and also, perhaps, an occasional suggestion for improvement. However, some points may be unjustified, or may be impracticable suggestions! Care is also needed that such informal contact does not weaken the command structure of the project and the authority of the immediate boss — this can arise if promises or decisions are made without proper consultation. Thus, whilst the staff should feel uninhibited about airing their views to the project manager, they should not be encouraged to by-pass their direct superiors on matters to be dealt with at that level.

Regular meetings of all staff should be held to keep staff in the picture about progress and changes to the objectives. These are also a safety valve for strongly held views, and they provide some collective relaxation which helps to promote a good team spirit; they are also evidence of good leadership.

(ii) Staff reviews

Management needs to make some tough decisions. For example, if a task is proving to be more difficult than envisaged, the decision may be either that the person is to be supported or is to be replaced. In considering the removal of an 'incompetent' person, it is useful to pose the question: 'which decision will cause the project to suffer more — retaining the person, or obtaining a replacement, given the uncertainty about the new person's capability?'

(iii) User rapport

It is often difficult to establish good rapport between project staff and the users of the system — particularly where there is a fixed-price contract, where there may be an adversarial attitude about the 'grey areas' in the requirements and the need for changes. The project manager should foster the relationship by arranging joint meetings to review progress and sensitive issues, such as the acceptance and introduction of the system. Even if such meetings generate criticism of the project and requests for changes, the project manager can still react positively without making premature commitments; for example, by listening to the arguments and demonstrating that staff understand the users' needs and, if there is doubt, by some further investigation.

(iv) Staff welfare

The project team is likely to be stretched, and exceptional effort and long hours are the norm on large projects. The pressures can be eased by arranging informal 'get togethers' — a pint at lunch time — or other means of generating some collective relaxation in the working environment. Consideration for the staff should also be reflected in their welfare; for example, refreshments and transport when staff work late hours and weekends.

(v) Project audits

The project manager, or the directing management, may arrange for an audit of the project by some independent and external authority as a safeguard for detecting and correcting major weaknesses. However, arranging an effective investigation is not easy and there are serious implications to be recognised.

An audit which aims to detect any major weakness should be carried out by extremely capable people, i.e. of higher professional level than the project management; otherwise, only defects of detail may emerge without exposing the fundamental weaknesses — and the directing management can be dangerously misled. The findings of an effective audit may recommend major and unpalatable action, involving back-tracking and excess cost, and there may be criticism of the project manager. Decisions about project audits thus need to be considered carefully at the the directing level, above the project manager, which should be prepared to act on unpalatable findings and make some tough decisions.

Conclusion

Throughout this chapter there has been continuous reference to the dependence on the project manager: firstly, at the macro level, in steering the course of the project and establishing a rapport with the purchaser and users; secondly, at the detailed technical level, in controlling the progress and quality of the development work; and finally, at the general management level, in leading and motivating the staff and controlling the use of resources. Thus the stage is set for the next chapter, which considers how such a paragon can be obtained, motivated and directed.

qualified person is not available; this may arise because, at the outset, there is only an uncertain and sketchy view of the job, making it difficult to appoint anyone other than an exceptional candidate with a proven record on similar projects. And a delayed appointment means that there will be a separate manager or leader of the initial design phase. However, it is important that the project manager is available in time to approve the design architecture, the project plan and costing, as emphasised in Chapters 3 and 4. There is therefore a limited window for the appointment; and it is assumed in this chapter that the selection is made in the latter half of the design stage when there is a reasonable understanding of the system and the main hazards.

If suitable candidates are not already available when the design is initiated, the limited window makes external recruitment very difficult; it may not even be possible if there is doubt as to whether the project proposal will be accepted — as is the case with competing contractors. Therefore, to be confident that the project manager will be appointed on time, purchasers are advised to check, at the outset, that a contractor does have ready access to a suitable candidate — this should even be a qualification for bidding for the project. And also the project manager should be approved by the purchaser.

It may not be easy to find someone who can vet the technical qualifications of the candidates because such a person needs at least comparable experience to that of the candidates. If this means that an outside body is required to fill that role, this person should be identified well beforehand in order to help in planning the recruitment process. Such a technical selector should also be involved, subsequently, in directing or advising the project manager, and to provide some accountability for the selection.

6.3   A summary of the selection process

Selecting a manager for any new job is difficult and especially so in this case where there is bound to be some uncertainty about the job and the risks. Yet, the selection should aim to match the job profile with the candidate's qualifications. It is therefore suggested that a key part of the selection process should focus on the specific challenges, as indicated in Figure 6.1. The selectors should prepare questions about the difficulties and uncertainties of the project; and then, with prior briefing of the candidate, the interview can assess the candidate's views and suggestions about how to make the project successful. This approach is described in the following sections, starting with the nature of a project manager's job.

6.4   The main characteristics of the role

The following summary of the role is in two parts: first the establishment of the project foundations; and then the management of the implementation.

6 The project manager

6.1 Introduction

The project manager has more influence than any other person on the success of the project, many of which have failed because the manager was not up to the job. On the other hand, a very able person can compensate for a weak foundation and steer a high risk project to a satisfactory result. Between these extremes, the capability of the manager has a considerable influence on the degree of success in meeting the project objectives, particularly the cost, timescale and the quality of the system. This relationship, between the manager's capability and the degree of success of the project, also explains why it is important that the manager personally endorses the design, plan and costing, as has been emphasised throughout the book.

Unfortunately, the selection process cannot be expected to predict how well the candidate will succeed in the job; and given that there is a world-wide shortage of managers who can direct large-scale projects, it is unusual to have the luxury of several well-qualified candidates. More commonly, the challenge is to identify one person who is willing, and can be trusted to do the job adequately. The consequences of an unsatisfactory appointment are serious — major delay or failure of the project — and even if an incompetent manager can be replaced during the project, the design and plan may have to be changed. The disruption will also be painful — both to the project and the career of the failed manager.

The selection process is the more hazardous because the role is largely isolated, and it is difficult to compensate for a manager's weakness. This need for self-sufficiency, coupled with tight budgets and timescale, does not allow much scope, either for mistakes in selection or for learning on the job.

This chapter addresses these problems by suggesting how the appointment process can be staged, and how the manager can be motivated and directed. It is relevant both for project managers and their directors and, because the suggestions are largely based on the nature of the role, there is also a summary of some key points from preceding chapters.

6.2 Appointment policy

Ideally, the project manager should direct both design and implementation phases, but the appointment is often delayed until late in the design phase because a

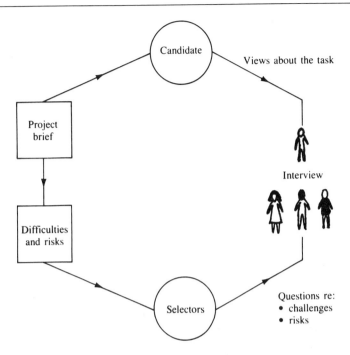

Figure 6.1 How to select the project manager

6.4.1 Building the project foundations

(i) Staffing

When the project is launched, it is unlikely that more than a small nucleus of staff will exist, and the outstanding positions need to be filled rapidly. Any key staff will have to be selected carefully because so much depends on their capability; they should therefore have a known track record on similar projects and, preferably, be known as past colleagues of the project manager.

The project manager will probably have a tough challenge if some of these senior staff have to be recruited within a short timescale, and much may depend on the manager's personal contacts with potential recruits. There may also be budgetary constraints which affect salary levels and the ability to hire contract staff. And, even if suitable staff exist within the corporate organisation, they may not be available to the project. (Incidentally, I have always found that competent hired staff are just as valuable and loyal to the project as permanent staff.)

(ii) The system design and project strategy

The project manager must be able to assess the system design, as described in Chapter 4, to identify weaknesses and to direct the necessary improvements; the manager must also be able to appraise changes to the design which arise as the project proceeds.

Even if the manager was involved in the design and planning stages, as was emphasised in Chapter 5, there should be a continuous review to check that the right task is being carried out — to ensure that the system will meet the real strategic and business needs of the purchaser. And although the responsibility for the system requirements lies strictly with the purchaser, the project manager can and should provide some safeguard against a belated realisation that the project does not meet the real business need. Much therefore depends on the strategic ability of the manager, and this dependence is greater the later the appointment — especially where the manager inherits a design proposal produced by others.

(iii) Plans and estimates

It has been strongly advocated throughout the book that the estimates should be based on a plan of the project activities, even though this involves a great deal of work. Given that the project manager does direct the planning process, this should provide some safeguard against cost and timescale over-runs. However, the manager also has to aim for an efficient and cost-effective result, and this is usually a tough challenge, especially where there is competitive bidding. And, as discussed in Chapter 4, much depends on the manager's ability to assess the risks in such a way that the directing management can make a sound decision about the objectives of timescale and cost.

(iv) Establishing the project environment

Much should have been done before the development work commences. Apart from the physical resources, such as the project accommodation and test equipment, the development standards and tools for improving the quality and productivity have to be determined. The preparations have to be tailored to match the project; some may even require special authorisation and investment, and yet they should be largely complete before launching the project because there is little time to develop new procedures or tools once the project is authorised. And since there is no common prescription for project standards, much depends on the past experience and judgement of the manager to avoid omissions and costly mistakes. For example, any plan to use new 'software engineering' tools should have investigated the extent of the learning curve and the possibility of teething problems.

(v) User interfaces

The importance of active involvement by the users cannot be emphasised too strongly and this depends on the inter-personal skills of the project manager. Arrangements need to be made for joint reviews at agreed milestones; there should be close liaison in activities which are related to the project but are not within its responsibility, such as the development of the user interface with the computer system and training the end-users and operators; and it is most important to agree the procedure for controlling changes to the design.

6.4.2 Managing the project

There are some general aspects of the project manager's role which are similar to those of other managers who have a constructive task with specific objectives — this applies to many new ventures. There are also similarities with any hazardous mission which needs self-reliant leadership. And the main challenge in computer projects is to overcome the inevitable hazards which arise. This requires both management ability and technical skill so that an active lead can be provided in solving major problems. For example, if part of the design is found to be impracticable, the selection of a sound alternative, of least cost and risk, should be influenced by the project manager's own judgement; and this may then have to be 'sold' to the purchaser and users and project staff. It is this mixture of general management and technical capability which is a key characteristic of managing computer projects.

6.5   Sizing the job

The selection of the manager needs to relate to the profile of the particular job. The 'size' of the job also indicates the level and value of the required manager. And the job can be partly gauged by the extent of the system and of the development task — both of which depend on the project budget. Thus a £10 million project is a bigger job than a £2 million one, but not by as much as five times because it is not a linear relationship. Furthermore, the cost of the development has more impact on the size of the job than the hardware cost. But there is also another important indicator — the difficulty of the job — as represented by the complexity, uncertainties and risks of the project. And, because the difficulty factor has such a great impact on the development cost, its influence on the size and challenge of the job should be gauged — even though this is tentative at that early point in the development when the project manager is to be selected.

One way of visualising the impact is shown in Figure 6.2. The curves indicate how the development cost of a project depends on the degree of its difficulty. Two curves are shown to reflect the uncertainty in forecasting the cost for a particular project — the upper curve is the conservative forecast, whilst the lower curve represents an optimistic view. And, because there is more uncertainty about the eventual cost of a more difficult project, the gap between the curves widens. Thus, for a pioneering project with a possible development cost of between £2 million and £3 million, there is a large (50 per cent) uncertainty factor of up to £1 million. The eventual cost depends on the design and plan, and on how the project is steered through the hazards; and thus much of the cost variance depends on the skill of the project manager. At the other extreme, Figure 6.2 indicates that, if the project had been straightforward, with few uncertainties and risk, the

Figure 6.2 Sizing the project and gauging how much depends on the project manager

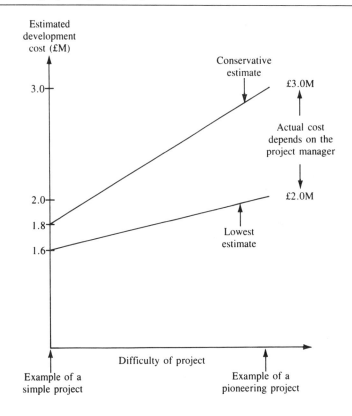

cost variance may have only ranged from £1.6 million to £1.8 million, and the task could have been carried out by a less capable manager.

The degree of project difficulty depends on assessing several factors, such as the following:

- any specific risk factors about the system and its development;
- system complexity, for example a distributed system or one with stringent reliability, resilience or performance requirements;
- timescale, i.e. the degree of tightness and criticality;
- user competence, i.e. poor ability or co-operation from the users will greatly add to the job challenge;
- project staffing, i.e. lack of available staff for the project or the need for a large or difficult recruitment campaign.

Although there is no formula for quantifying these factors, each contributes to an overall prediction of the difficulty factor and project cost. And the degree of uncertainty of each factor contributes to the gap between the overall upper and lower forecasts; for example, the need to hire contract staff as opposed to permanent staff. (These factors are also used in assessing the job candidates, as shown in Section 6.7.)

6.6   Skills profile

The more important attributes of a successful project manager can be summarised succinctly in just the following three qualifications:

(a)   relevant past experience of project management;
(b)   technical problem solving ability;
(c)   management ability.

These may be the headline qualifications when searching for candidates prior to interviews and, subsequently, when assessing their suitability for the job. Each is considered further below:

(a)   Experience. Since most lessons can only be learned in a practical context, it is essential that the manager has appropriate experience of leading a similar computer project. However, this may be somewhat smaller than the project being considered — to allow those younger managers to be considered who naturally seek a more challenging job than was their previous role.
(b)   Technical problem solving. As discussed in Section 6.4, the manager needs to have sufficient intellectual and technical ability to be able to perceive the major pitfalls, and to take the lead, where necessary, in proposing and justifying solutions.
(c)   Management capability. The challenge of getting things done, via the efforts of others, was considered in Chapter 5. It needs a single-minded and determined dedication to succeed in the face of many difficulties; and this requires a fairly rare blend of 'street-wise' toughness and negotiating skill, but not 'tunnel vision', when dealing with complex issues. The manager has to harness and motivate both project staff and sub-contractors, and obtain the co-operation of the end-users, success being signified by earning the respect of both staff and customer.

In addition to the above qualifications, the manager has to be personally acceptable and trusted by the directing authority, and be able to remain with a project of long duration until completion.

6.7   Selection methods

Although various selection techniques may be useful, such as psychological and intelligence tests where the candidate is not well known, one of the most powerful tests is pragmatic — judging the candidate's reaction to some of the main decisions and challenges which actually affect the project.

   The suggested approach is partly based on the candidate's own assessment of the job to be done. This requires that the applicants are briefed in advance of the interview about the project and the design work to date. The briefing, plus a set of prepared questions, are used to stimulate the candidate's own views about the project; for example, the applicant's views about the practicality of the proposed timescale should reveal much about his or her capability to do the job.

It is appreciated that such an approach is not always possible; there may be security restrictions on the release of project information, or the candidates may not be able to devote sufficient time to such preparations. However, in such cases, the technical selector should be able to devise a similar or hypothetical project to reveal sufficient evidence about the candidate's capability.

The following examples of questions to be put to the candidate during the interview are similar to the tasks described in Section 6.4 for preparing for the project; and they also relate to the 'difficulties', identified in Section 6.5, for 'sizing' the project:

- staffing, i.e. how to obtain the chief subordinates;
- project strategy, i.e. assessment of the major hazards and suggestions about the strategic approach;
- estimating, i.e. the approach to be used for estimating the costs and timescales and quantifying the risks;
- project environment and standards, i.e. the policy to be adopted for quality control;
- user interface, i.e. the approach to be taken in establishing user involvement;
- problem solving ability, i.e. the approach for solving the identified problems and for any other unexpected problems;
- controlling progress, i.e. the method for reviewing progress and for reporting upwards.

In addition to these questions, the manager's past record should be reviewed — especially past experience of managing other projects. And, where the candidate is not known to the selectors, views should be sought from several references.

6.8 Motivation

Given the risks and uncertainties in any large project, the project manager has to be highly motivated to succeed — in particular to complete the project at the lowest possible cost and shortest timescale. It is therefore worth while to consider whether the manager's effectiveness can be increased by some financial incentive to achieve and to beat the targets; this could be based on a bonus package which measures the actual project achievement against set targets of both expenditure and timescale. However, there are some pitfalls and precautions which need to be covered, as indicated below:

- Safeguards are needed to ensure that quality is not sacrificed; there may be penalty points for not fully meeting a requirement such as poor software quality.
- Changes to the system requirements, and hence to the size of the task, may not be fairly reflected in the bonus criteria; for example, changes which are not attributable to the purchaser have to be borne by the project, and the timescale may be unchanged although the task becomes much more difficult.
- Imprecise acceptance criteria or lack of objective measures will make it difficult to determine the completion of the entire project or of intermediate milestones.

If such difficulties are not avoided, *ad hoc* decisions made during the project about how the bonus scheme is affected may upset the project manager, and may make the scheme impracticable or even demotivating. In such circumstances, it is better not to have a bonus scheme at all than to have one which is badly flawed.

6.9   Direction of the project manager

Most of the high level decisions will have been made by the time the project is committed. And, by and large, the project manager should then be given a free hand to get on with the job, subject to limits of authority such as approval of major changes and submission of progress reports and reviews. However, some guidance is required since few people are completely self-sufficient, particularly a younger person, who may be capable but somewhat over-stretched. Such guidance may also reduce the risk of having to replace a manager.

6.9.1   Ad hoc guidance

In a major project, no amount of guidance can compensate for inadequate basic ability in the project manager; for example, it is not practicable to supervise a project manager closely without diluting the authority of that person's role and respect of the team. In effect, the supervisor would become the real project manager, but possibly without being able to spare enough time, and the so-called 'project manager' would become an assistant or deputy. Thus guidance for an effective project manager should be strictly limited to regular reviews and abnormal circumstances, such as the following:

- User rapport. Communication between the project manager and the purchasing authority is sometimes unsatisfactory and causes mistrust or conflict.
- Major problems. Help or advice is not always sought when needed, even though the manager is struggling. The technical director or advisor should therefore build up a rapport with the project manager, via regular monitoring of progress, in order to identify when help is needed.
- Negotiations with the purchaser. Difficulties may arise which are outside the control of the manager; for example, there may be poor co-operation by the purchaser's staff or by a contractor to the purchaser.

6.9.2   Project reviews

The periodical reviews should not only investigate the progress of the project in relation to the objectives, they should also be used to monitor the performance of the project manager and to discern where guidance is needed. It is therefore important that the directing management is qualified to appraise the project reports and the key issues arising in the progress reviews.

If the directing management is not sufficiently technical, some other person(s) should be involved as the technical advisor(s), even if hired from a third party such as a consultancy firm. The advisor(s) may also provide technical guidance to the project manager as previously described.

The reviews should cover the following subjects:

- progress to-date of the activities compared with the plan, and explanations of discrepancies and corrective action;
- changes and their impact on the plan;
- expansion of plans for later project stages, such as preparation for system acceptance and introduction;
- forecasting future progress;
- staff procurement problems;
- user liaison, i.e. concerns relating to the purchaser and end-users;
- costs to date and the forecast compared with a phased budget, and an account of any differences.

From such reviews, the directing authority should be able to judge the state of the project and whether any exceptional action is needed as a follow-up.

6.9.3 Summary

In reviewing progress, there is often an unspoken undercurrent which influences the attitudes of the reporting managers. This may exist because a manager is reluctant to reveal some undisclosed problem or concern. One such 'problem' which commonly arises is where the manager feels that it is premature to raise the issue until its impact is clearer; this is not necessarily reprehensible, since premature revelation of problems without positive recommendations often causes unnecessary alarm and negative reactions. However, it is a matter of fine judgement as to when a problem should be brought to the attention of a higher level — on balance it is better to be more frank than less in regard to any potential major problem so that it does not emerge at short notice when it may have very damaging impact.

This hidden agenda emphasises the need for perceptive and sensitive monitoring of progress by the directing authority above the project manager. And perhaps the key to successful direction is whether there is mutual trust and respect among all the managers and other principal parties — this is also the hallmark for the successful project.

7 Conclusion

Following the preceding coverage of the more crucial aspects of managing large computer projects, some conclusions can now be drawn to add to the overall perspective.

There has been a lot of emphasis on the need for sound foundations — the design architecture and, especially, the project plan, to back up a realistic prediction of the timescale and resources, and to get the project on to a sound basis. Such careful preparation is vital for a successful project, but this will only happen if the team, and especially the project manager, are qualified for the job. If the challenge exceeds their abilities, the foundations will be weak. On the other hand, a capable manager can establish a sound project, despite major obstacles such as commercial pressures and deadlines, both for the proposal and for completing the project.

Hence, much depends on the development of project management skills in both the technical and the more general aspects of the role. However, there also has to be sufficient inherent aptitude and experience — hence the emphasis on careful selection. An example of a vital leadership skill is the need to influence the non-technical decision-makers, the purchaser, the users and the directing management so that they all accept what needs to be done to make the project successful. And for this to happen, the project manager has to ensure, perhaps with some diplomacy, that they understand the key issues, even if the decision-makers have little or no technical knowledge.

The technical management of many projects has suffered somewhat from gaps in understanding those aspects of project planning and control highlighted in this book. More needs to be learned by feedback from project experience, yet projects are often regarded as one-off ventures with scant regard for learning how they could have been better managed. These lessons emphasise the need to supplement individual experience so that the project manager is proficient, and is confident about handling the basic tasks — then the particular challenges of a project can receive the main attention. Hopefully, this book makes some contribution towards that aim.

Appendix   Estimating guidelines

A.1   Introduction

A practical method is described for estimating the staffing costs and timescales of a large project. The method is focused mainly on the software since this is the critical task, and it is assumed that the planning approach is followed as described in Chapter 4. However, since this Appendix may be read independently of that chapter, the principles are briefly re-stated.

The need to produce estimates as soon as possible, before too much time is spent on the design and planning work, has led to the development of several theoretical methods. They can be used early in the development cycle, even before an implementation plan has been produced, and most methods are incorporated in computerised models for making the calculations. However, although these methods are used widely, especially for preliminary estimates, they are limited in producing a reliable and firm estimate.

The 'planned method' described here follows a different approach from the modelling methods; the estimate is based on a plan of how the project will be implemented and this approach, although requiring much more effort than using a model, has the following benefits:

- The existence of the plan generates *confidence* that the estimator understands how the job can be done, and is motivated to achieve the plan.
- If the plan is endorsed by the designated project manager, it reflects a *commitment* as to how the project will actually be carried out.
- The plan identifies the need for *quality* control and re-work activity since this consumes around half of the project effort.
- The plan identifies the uncertainties and *risks* and their impact on both cost and timescale.

A.2   The scope of the estimate

The estimate is assessed separately in the following three categories to reflect the different nature of the work:

1. Programming tasks. These cover the main productive work which converts the architectural design into tested programs. The programs are assumed to

be written in a high level language, although the same principles, if not the detail, would apply if either low level or macro languages were used.

2. System tasks. These cover the integration and test of the complete system and its introduction to live operation and acceptance by the purchaser.

3. Management, supporting and ancillary tasks. The support tasks include quality assurance and project administration and the ancillary tasks include the production of deliverables, such as manuals and user training.

The above tasks should all be defined within the Work Breakdown Structure, as shown in Chapter 4, so that there is a definitive check list of all work to be carried out.

Figure A.1 indicates the overall staffing profile and how the staff in each category varies over the project duration. The more important and difficult estimates are for the two 'productive' categories, the programming and system

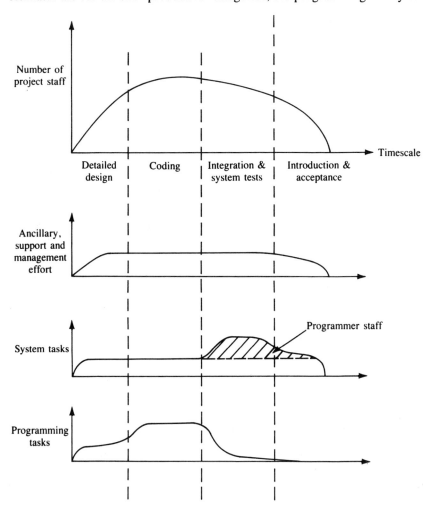

Figure A.1 Staff profiles

work, which are described in more detail below; the estimates of the other tasks are only briefly considered since they are largely based on the estimates of the 'productive' work. The shaded portion of the staff profile, for the system tasks, represents the need to use programming staff for correcting the software errors which emerge during the integration and system testing.

A.2.1   *The programming tasks*

These cover the two successive stages — detailed design and coding — which are considered as one category since there is continuity of staffing, although there is a junction between the stages, for the inspection and approval of the design.

The detailed design begins with the expansion of the architectural design, and ends after approval of specifications for the coding and testing of the program modules. The boundaries of the coding and unit testing are defined by the completion of the detailed design and the successful conclusion of the unit tests.

A.2.2   *The system tasks*

These tasks are somewhat diverse as is indicated below:

- updating the design proposal for changes and clarifications in liaison with the users and programmers;
- planning and conducting the integration and testing of the system;
- planning and achieving the acceptance and introduction of the system;
- planning and carrying out any implementation tasks other than the programming work, including preparation for the installation, use and support of the system.

The integration and system testing is the largest of these tasks — it may require up to about half of the total project resource. The tests also occupy much of this Appendix since there is little guidance in the literature about how to plan the tests, and a method is suggested which is based on the impact of software defects.

Since it is inevitable that there will be residual defects after system testing, the correction of software defects continues well into the live use of the system, and therefore the timescale to attain satisfactory operational reliability is an important part of the project. For example, if a project completes system testing on schedule after twelve months, but then requires a further six months to achieve a satisfactory operational state, the real duration of the project should be regarded as eighteen months.

A.2.3   *Support and ancillary work*

Apart from the overhead tasks which support the productive work of the project, this category includes the ancillary deliverables, such as the training of user staff and the production of user manuals and maintenance aids. An indication of the items and activities is given in the work breakdown summary in Chapter 4, and also in Section A.12 at the end of this Appendix.

The plans for producing the ancillaries, and for establishing the project support environment, need to be carefully co-ordinated with the productive work since there are some important inter-dependencies. For example, the project standards should be available before programming begins, and the operating manuals should be drafted before completion of the detailed design so that the man-machine interface is fully and accurately reflected in the detailed specifications.

A.3 Some basic characteristics of the estimate

In addition to the two main dimensions of the estimate, the timescale and the staffing cost, the following assessment also covers the other substantial resource, the computing test facility.

A.3.1 Staffing costs and timescales

The staffing profile of a project resembles that shown in Figure A.1, where the peak level occurs during the coding stage. And, although the staffing and timescale are mainly affected by the size and difficulty of the programs to be produced, there are many other influences which are described in detail by B. Boehm (1981) and C. Jones (1986).

A project is often constrained to achieve a deadline completion, but a planned timescale cannot easily be contracted and it may not be possible to meet the target. This arises because there is no simple linear relationship between staffing and timescale — it is not possible to complete the job in half the time by doubling the staff. The implications of varying the staffing are as described below:

1. Increasing the staffing. This compresses the timescale by a limited amount but it also escalates the cost, mainly because there are more concurrent activities which increase the difficulty of controlling the work and which require more overhead resource for checks, co-ordination and supervision. The actual impact on the cost and timescale depends much on the particular activities affected, and on the skill levels of the extra staff; but, in practice, due to the limited availability of highly skilled staff, the minimum timescale is unlikely to be much less than about 70—80 per cent of what was initially proposed as a cost-effective target.

2. Reducing the staffing. This usually lengthens the timescale, but the cost may be increased or reduced, depending on the particular circumstances. For example, if the coding staff is reduced from, say, ten to six by eliminating all inexperienced staff, the timescale may only be extended slightly and the cost will be reduced. On the other hand, if the highly skilled staff working on the detailed design are reduced from four to two, leaving a weak coverage of skills, the timescale will be more than doubled and the cost will increase.

(Note. Such conclusions expose a particular limitation of estimating models, and some models give widely different predictions for altering the staffing and timescale relationship; this may occur because the impact is assessed at the overall project level, whereas, as shown above, the relationship may be different in each stage and it also depends on the specific skills which are used.)

A.3.2   Project support and ancillary staffing

This depends on the particular project environment and the extent of the system; for example, a system which is to be dispersed over a large number of sites will need more documentation and more user training than that for a single computer centre. Consequently, the support and ancillary staffing may vary between about one-quarter and one-half of the total staffing.

A.3.3   Non-staffing costs

The main item is the computing facility for testing the system under development. The hardware in the test bed may be less extensive than in the operational system, but it should have similar components, and these should replicate the crucial interfaces with the bespoke software. The test capacity may be gradually expanded during the project to meet the increasing volume of testing; but there should always be sufficient capacity to avoid slippage of the development timescale because the marginal cost of extra hardware should be much less than the cost of a project delay. The test system may also be used by the software tools for configuration and management control of the project and for the designers and coders.

The hardware configuration in the system test should be an 'adequate' representation of the full operational system. And the significance of any shortfall of equipment or test data should be assessed by the particular impact on the tests to be carried out; these tests aim to match the system requirement as far as is practicable, but there are usually some limitations, such as the size of the test data-base, the volume of test data, and the full extent of peripheral and terminal equipment.

It is not easy to predict the amount of testing time which is required throughout the development. However, apart from the final stage of system testing, which is considered below, the test resource is not normally critical, assuming that sufficient computing power can be made available. A rough indication of the overall use of computer time is given in the literature, about three computer hours per man-month of development effort is a possible rough average (Boehm 1981), but such a yardstick is based on a very wide spread of historical data. Furthermore, wide variations in the amount of testing, from project to project, are to be expected, even for similar projects, because there are many uncertain variables; for example, differences in the power of the test system, in the complexity of the system and, above all, in the quality of the development work.

Some guidance on the amount of machine time for system testing is provided by a yardstick of the average computer time used for correcting each software fault which arises during the test (see Section A.10). Such a yardstick is useful since the bulk of the test resource is spent on error correction.

A.4 An outline of the approach

A.4.1 Basic principles

The early planning work, which determined the development strategy, is assumed to have been completed as described in Chapter 4. The detailed planning then continues until the development work has been dissected into small activities which can be gauged in such terms as: 'this activity should take J.Smith X days to accomplish'. The tasks involved in each activity, together with the allocated resources, should be defined and recorded within a 'work package', as described in Chapter 4, so that there is no ambiguity about what has to be done. (A work package may cover one or more activities.)

The planning can be carried out in two steps: firstly, a rough, initial version of the plan is produced which identifies the activities; secondly, the staffing and timescale are estimated for each activity, and these are then aggregated to produce the overall estimates.

A.4.2 The initial plan

This should provide a practical view of how the task can be achieved — by identifying the activities and their inter-relationship, and presenting them in some organised form. The plan should be supported by the work packages, and each of these should specify the resources and tasks for a related group of activities. And, although the initial plan should depict all activities, it is dimensionless until the estimating has been carried out in the next planning step.

Figure A.2 illustrates a skeleton organisation of the work for part of the detailed design stage, involving eleven activities for one sub-system.

A.4.3 Staffing estimate

The most crucial task is to determine the effort required to accomplish each activity. And it should be possible to make reliable judgements if the activities are small, such that each requires no more than a few man-weeks of effort; the reliability of the estimate will be further improved if the estimator is also the person who will be responsible for the work. But special care is needed in this 'bottom-up' approach to take full account of the overheads, such as those described below, because historically the allowance has often been grossly inadequate and has been a major cause of some optimistic estimates:

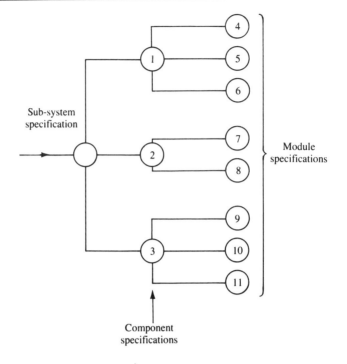

(i) The work overhead

- Associated tasks such as documentation and quality checks. Because these differ at each stage in the project, they should be specified in the relevant work packages.
- Time spent in communicating with other staff, and with users, in connection with the job. This also varies at each stage, and increases the larger the project.
- Unproductive time, which is not connected with the work in hand, including technical reading, personal matters and even idle chat. This can take as much as 25 per cent of the total time and depends on staff motivation and management control.

(ii) The staff overhead

This covers all absences from the place of work, including training, holidays, travel, etc. The allowance may be deducted from the calendar year to leave about forty-two weeks of effective work for permanent staff (but this may be forty-six weeks or more for hired staff who have less absences); and there will be a further reduction if much travelling is involved. The average impact of this overhead can be represented by increasing each activity estimate by, say, 25 per cent. But the specific impact of a lengthy holiday absence of a key staff member needs to be assessed in case it affects a critical path of the project.

The work packages should also specify the type and level of skill to be used, and its phasing if more than one person is involved. From such a profile, both staffing and timescale can be calculated, as shown in the following example:

Staff required for Activity X:

Designer P1 for 7 man-weeks
Programmer P2 for 3 man-weeks in the latter part of the activity

Total effort = 10 man-weeks
Duration of activity = 7 weeks

The above example is also shown in Figure A.3, which is discussed below.

A.4.4   The planning and estimating sequence

Since the process is similar for all stages, a possible sequence of steps is described below and is illustrated in Figure A.3.

Step A. Defining and organising the work

The work in each stage may be defined as a hierarchy of work packages, as shown in the diagram, and/or by a provisional network of the activities, as shown in Figure A.2. (For illustrative purposes, it is assumed in Figure A.3 that a work package contains only one activity.)

Step B. Estimating the size of the work

The effort, to accomplish each activity, is expressed in man-days or weeks and is translated into a timescale by relating the effort to the staffing profile, as shown in the diagram and in the above example.

Step C. The activity plan

The timed activities are formed into a PERT type of network which identifies the inter-dependencies and critical paths. This network indicates the overall timescale for the project which can then be adjusted by iteration of steps B and C.

Step D. The staffing schedule

Producing a 'week by week' staffing schedule, as shown in Figure A.3, reveals the staff profile throughout the project. The schedule can be modified until the staffing is at a practical and cost-effective level where the staff are fully utilised; this will involve some iteration of the activity plans and their resourcing. The completed schedule then provides the basis for the costing and recruitment plans.

Figure A.3 Planning
and estimating steps

STEP A   Work breakdown structure

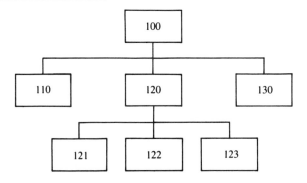

STEP B   Staffing estimate

| | Work packages | | |
Staff	121	122	123 ...
P_1	7	6	
P_2	3	—	
.			
.			
.			
Man-weeks	10	6	
Timescale (weeks)	7	6	

STEP C   Activity plan

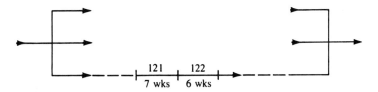

STEP D   Staff schedule

| | Week number | | | |
Staff	1 ...	7 ...	13 ...	
P_1		121		
P_2			121	
.				
.				
.				
P_n				
Staff total				

A.4.5 Risk assessment

The uncertainties in estimating can be expressed in the following manner:

(i) The timescale

Any uncertainty about the duration of activities, particularly the critical paths, can be quantified by setting early and late finish dates; these can then be summarised to predict the earliest and latest completion of the overall project. The early date may be defined as that which is achievable if there are no unexpected difficulties and if other factors are favourable, such as the ready availability of skilled staff and development tools; such a forecast is therefore a high risk with around a 50/50 chance of achievement. On the other hand, the late forecast should include contingencies which justify a high degree of confidence, at least at a 90 per cent level, that completion will occur before that date.

The results may be presented in two separate activity plans in order to present a clear picture of the two extreme scenarios.

(ii) The resources

The cost estimates for each timescale should reflect any significant uncertainties in the cost of resources, especially if the resource does not already exist; this applies to recruitment and salary costs, to the hiring cost of contract staff and to any contracted machine testing. The uncertainty may be reflected in two costings for each timescale limit; the lower level of cost will then represent the most optimistic cost and the upper level will depict the conservative view.

(iii) Summary

The results for each category of task can be expressed in the following manner:

- Optimistic timescale:
    lowest cost;
    highest cost.
- Conservative timescale:
    lowest cost;
    highest cost.

It is assumed that the directing authority, to whom the project manager reports, will review such an assessment and set specific objectives for the cost and timescale — probably somewhere between these limits.

A.5 The programming tasks

These expand the architectural design until the coded modules are produced and tested. A large system is usually divided from the highest level into sub-systems which may be further broken down into intermediate 'components' before the program modules are specified. Each component needs to be assessed separately since it will have a unique degree of difficulty; and, preferably, the estimate should be produced by the person who is going to be responsible for the activity.

(Note. The ability to distribute the responsibility for estimating among several people with a linked accountability should improve the reliability of the estimate. Unfortunately this cannot apply to the system test stage, which depends on the collective effort of the project team.)

Figure A.4 illustrates the outline of a programming plan for a sub-system which has eight concurrent components, two of which are shown as expanded into nine modules for coding. This outline should be fully expanded in Step A of the planning process, so that all activities are identified. This diagram also highlights the 'critical paths' — the activities which determine the timescale for completing a related group of activities before the subsequent group can commence.

Figure A.4 Outline of a programming activity plan

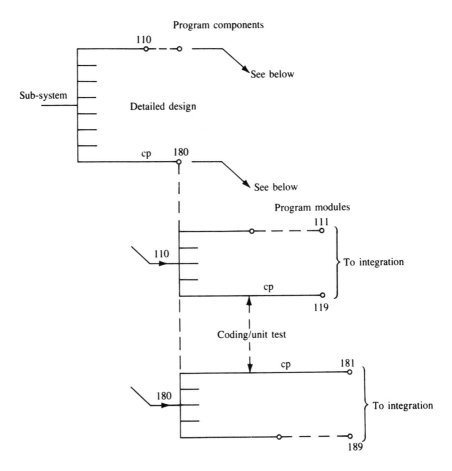

Key: cp — critical path

A.6   The detailed design stage

The following description should be read in conjunction with the steps illustrated in Figure A.3.

Step A. Organisation of the work

This should show the activities to expand the sub-systems down to module specifications which will generate not more than a few hundred program statements. The tasks in each design activity, including documentation and inspections, should be identified in a work package covering one or more related activities.

Step B. Estimating the size of the work

The amount of the design effort depends so much on the particular designer that the estimator should be someone who can be trusted to have a realistic appreciation of what is involved and of how it can actually be accomplished. And, to reduce the complexity of estimating, the initial estimate may assume the use of a single person for each activity; this resource can then be increased later, if necessary, to achieve a shorter timescale.

Apart from depending on the skill level, the effort will be roughly proportional to the size of the programs to be produced — the number of coded instructions or program modules. (Alternatively, the size may be gauged using other ways such as the approach developed by Albrecht (see Albrecht and Gaffney 1983) which assesses the extent of the work by examining the so-called 'Function Points' — the number of inputs, outputs, enquiries, files and interfaces.)

The estimate also depends on two other assessments, as follows:

1. The nature of the system, its complexity and novelty, and any aids and constraints which may expedite or impede the work. For example, it may be important to achieve a streamlined response time.
2. The project capability. Apart from the skill level, other influences on productivity are the tools, aids and development constraints, such as project standards and test facilities.

It is necessary to make a combined assessment of all these variables since they are interactive; for example, a difficult task for one person may be relatively easy for someone else. This composite variable can be regarded as the 'degree of difficulty' of the task for the person to whom it is assigned, and this may be quantified within the range from, say, one for an easy task to five for the most difficult. The estimating process for Step B in Figure A.3 may then be shown as in Table A.1.

To improve the reliability of the estimate, any activity with a longer duration than one or two months should be re-examined for further dissection to a lower level. A check should also be made that the estimates allow for the following overheads, as described in Section A.4.

Table A.1   Recording the estimate of the detailed design

Activity	Modules	Person	Difficulty	Man-weeks	Duration
X	10	A	3	8	8 wks.
Y	12	B	2	6	6 wks.
Etc.					

(i) Work overheads

- Quality. This should reflect the project standards, the methodology to be followed, the inspection of the detailed specifications and the subsequent corrections and verification. An allowance of around 25 per cent of the productive effort is suggested for the inspections and re-work in this stage.
- Associated documentation. Allowance should be made for producing documents, such as user and training manuals, in addition to the module, database and test specifications.
- Communication. Provision is required for 'hidden' communications such as queries, clarifications, explanations and discussions with other staff and with users.
- The unproductive and 'idle' time factor.

(ii) Staff overheads

The gross staffing level for each activity should be uplifted by the assessed amount for expected absences.

Step C. Planning the activities

After re-forming the network with the 'sized' activities, the critical paths will be apparent and the timescale for the stage can be calculated. If the staffing has to be increased to reduce the timescale, the impact can be gauged as shown in Figure A.3, where the addition of the second person, P2, only reduces the duration of activity 121 by one week, although the effort is increased by nearly 50 per cent.

Step D. Staff scheduling

The schedule, as in step D in Figure A.3, can be refined to optimise the staffing efficiency and to match the number of staff which can be obtained.

A.7   Coding and unit testing

Coding may commence before all detailed specifications have been produced, but not before all 'related' design work has been completed and approved; this means that coding should only be initiated when its parent specification will not be changed by any outstanding design of other sub-systems.

The planning of this stage should be co-ordinated with that of the next (integration) stage; then part of integration can begin immediately, after completing the unit testing for a particular group of modules.

Referring again to Figure A.3, the planning steps are as follows:

Step A. Organisation of the work

The extent of each activity should be made small enough for reliable estimating; for example, it may cover both coding and inspection of a group of related modules, with the unit test being regarded as a separate activity. The tasks within each activity, together with the criteria for its completion, should then be defined in the relevant work packages.

Step B. Estimating the size of the work

As for the detailed design, the estimate depends on the forecast size of the programs and on the variables — the system complexity and the project capability. A combined value of these variables may be regarded as the 'level of difficulty' of the task, and this is used to determine the productivity, expressed in instructions per man-week. This level is likely to be within the range of about 50–250 lines of high level source instructions per man-week (excluding comments and blanks), assuming the use of competent coders; the lower rates apply to complex real-time programs, and the highest rates refer to straightforward commercial programs. The effort, in man-weeks, for each activity is then calculated by dividing the estimated number of program instructions by the productivity.

(Note. Particular care is needed when referring to published yardsticks, since they may not be well defined. For example, productivity depends on the programming language and the size of the modules; it also depends on the scope of the work, and on whether inspections and other work and staff overheads are included.)

Although the coding rate of different people varies widely, an average level has to be assumed at this time if the actual staffing is not known. However, such an approximation can still produce a reliable estimate for a large project, given that the project manager is able to control progress and compensate for differences among the individual rates.

The example given in Table A.2 shows how an estimate may be recorded. These estimates should incorporate the following overheads, as more fully described in Section A.4:

Table A.2 Estimating coding and unit testing

Activity	Modules	Difficulty	No. instns.	Code rate	Man-weeks
X	10	3	1200	100/wk.	12
Y	12	2	1500	150/wk.	10

- Work overheads, i.e. for documentation and communication, especially for interfacing with other modules and resolving queries; for unproductive and idle time; and for inspections and re-working — this alone can take up about one-third of the work effort.
- Staff overheads, i.e. normal absences, excluding travel, for holidays and sickness require about 25 % to be added to the work effort (including the work overheads) over a full year.

The timescale of each activity is calculated, as shown in Step B in Figure A.3, by dividing the total man-weeks by the effective number of applied staff.

Step C. Planning the activities

The completed chart of the inter-linked activities will indicate the overall timescale and also the critical paths, which need to be adjusted if the timescale has to be reduced. The risks and uncertainties can then be quantified by setting the earliest and latest finish dates.

Step D. Scheduling resources and finalising the estimate

This involves producing a schedule of the staff required each week or month, and this may need adjustment to achieve a practicable and efficient staffing.

A.8   The integration and system tests

A.8.1   A simplified representation

The two successive tasks, of integrating the program modules and testing the overall system, both rely on incremental sub-tests. Consequently, a similar approach is taken in estimating both tests, and the common principles are described in this section. The approach is based on using a simple and rather crude model which is easy to construct and use. (A more comprehensive analysis and model of the process is described by Musa *et al.*, 1987.)

The model assumes that, in both integration and system testing, each test increment achieves a measurable milestone within the overall test and contains two different and concurrent activities, as shown in Figure A5. The upper line represents the activity of those system staff who conduct the test and detect the problems; this work is usually carried out by a small, dedicated team, although there may be separate teams for the integration and system testing. The lower line in the diagram represents the effort of the programmers who correct the detected faults — and who are usually only involved on a part-time basis.

(Note. The faults arising during the test are caused by defects in the system, but as most of these are software errors, the terms 'error' and 'defect' are used with the same meaning.)

The strongest intensity of each activity, indicated by the solid line, may be

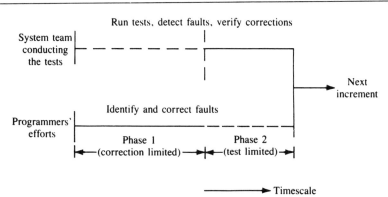

Figure A.5 The concurrent activities in a test increment

regarded as the 'critical' path of the test because this governs the overall rate of progress through each of the following test phases:

Phase 1   correction-limited phase. The majority of the defects are detected during the initial part of the test, and the correction work is assumed to dominate this phase of the test.

Phase 2   test-limited phase. This phase is entered when most of the defects have been corrected, and progress is then limited by the time for assurance testing and verifying the results.

The estimating process is simplified by assuming that only the dominating or critical activity determines the timescale in each phase. Thus an approximate timescale for Phase 2 is the idealised time to conduct the scheduled tests, without interruption for fault clearance, but including the preparation of the runs and verification of the results.

The timescale for Phase 1 is more difficult to predict. It depends on the number of defects and the rate of correction. However, a rough estimate can be obtained by constructing a visual model of the test activity, as shown by the graph in the upper part of Figure A.6. This indicates how software errors may be detected and corrected during each test increment, and it shows how the approximate duration of Phase 1 is given by dividing the total number of errors by the average number corrected each day. The lower part of Figure A.6 indicates how the correcting effort varies during the test and shows the average number of correcting staff which is used in forecasting the test duration. An example of the calculation is as follows:

Forecast number of errors $E = 50$
Average effort to correct one error, $N = 1$ man-day
Average correcting effort used each day, $S = 5$ staff
Average number of errors corrected each day $= (N \times S) = 5$
Timescale $= E/(N \times S) = 10$ days

This method requires some difficult judgements to be made — of the number of errors, the average rate of correction and the average number of correcting staff — but the following guidelines should be of some assistance.

Figure A.6 The estimating basis for system testing

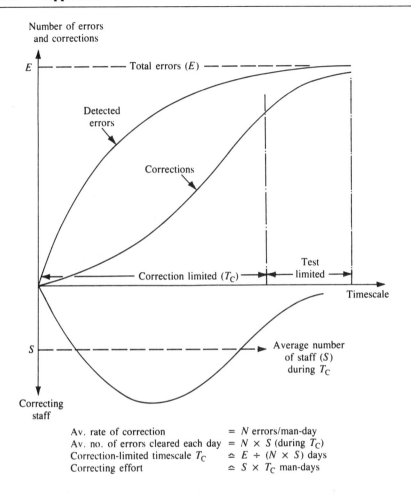

Av. rate of correction   = N errors/man-day
Av. no. of errors cleared each day = $N \times S$ (during T_C)
Correction-limited timescale T_C ≃ $E \div (N \times S)$ days
Correcting effort   ≃ $S \times T_C$ man-days

A.8.2 Error levels

The three yardsticks are somewhat speculative, and should be used cautiously as they are based on a limited amount of historical data. However, they do reflect several published indications and should at least help to supplement experienced judgement. (The same yardsticks, with the source references, are given in Chapter 5 to assist in the management control of the project.)

1. The overall number of errors. For most systems this is likely to be in the range of 20–50 per 1 K line of source code (KLOC), given good quality control, with inspections of both design and code. The actual number of errors is influenced by several factors, as discussed in Chapter 5 — more will occur in systems of high complexity and where there are many post-design changes, but there will be fewer if there are disciplined procedures and documentation.

2. The 'error removal profile'. This is fully described in Chapter 5; it is a prediction of the errors generated, and how they are removed by the various

tests and inspections, especially the inspections of the design and the coding. And, if these inspections are stringent, it is possible to remove about 75 per cent of the total errors prior to integration testing — leaving between about five and fourteen errors per KLOC at that point in the development.

3. The residual errors. After the system test, it is likely that between about 1.5 and 4.0 errors per KLOC will remain; and most of these should be detected during the early part of operational running. (Thus it is assumed that between about three and ten errors per KLOC will be detected in the integration and system tests.)

An example of an error forecast for a hypothetical system is as follows:

Total errors generated in design and coding = 40
Errors removed prior to integration testing @ 75% = 30
Errors remaining = 10
Target of residual errors after system testing = 3
Errors to be cleared in the integration and system tests = 7

(All the above figures relate to KLOC so that the total number is proportional to the size of the software.)

Further guidelines on estimating, together with more detailed examples, are given in the sections dealing separately with the integration tests and the system tests (Sections A.9 and A.10). And, although the suggested approach does involve difficult judgements, it should yield a more reliable forecast than can be obtained by other 'simpler' methods. One such method is described below, and this is examined to suggest how it may be used most effectively — perhaps to provide a preliminary or rough ball-park estimate.

A.8.3 A rough ball-park estimate

The effort for the integration and system test is assumed to be a 'rule of thumb' yardstick of a given percentage of the effort used in the preceding stages. However, published yardsticks vary substantially and they are often not well-defined; for example, for large systems with more than 100 K program statements, various published figures indicate that the test effort may be anywhere between about 30 and 120 per cent of that for the detailed design and coding.

To understand what affects this percentage ratio, we will first consider the idealised case where there are no errors; the testing effort will then be minimal and it will depend on the scope and depth of the tests; the effort increases with the size and complexity of the system, and with the required intensity of testing. However, in the 'real world of errors', the test effort will tend to escalate as the errors increase until, in the extreme case, where the quality of the programs is very poor, there are so many errors that correction completely dominates the activities, and progress is virtually brought to a standstill because the test is uncontrollable.

The impact of such circumstances is roughly illustrated in Figure A.7, which shows how the minimum test effort corresponds to the ideal case of zero errors,

Figure A.7 Impact of
errors on integration
and system test effort

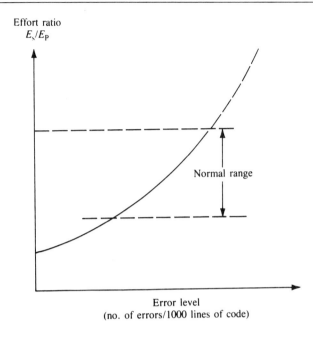

Effort ratio
E_s/E_P

Normal range

Error level
(no. of errors/1000 lines of code)

E_s — staffing for integration and system tests
E_P — staffing for programming work

and also how the timescale escalates towards infinity as the error rate increases. The scale and shape of the graph will vary somewhat for different projects, being affected to some extent by factors other than the error level, such as the depth and extent of the tests. However, these other factors also influence the error rate, which is believed to be the single most important variable. This assumption appears to be justified because its wide spread is comparable with the assumed range of effort ratios; for example, the suggested range of error levels of between three and ten per KLOC is similar to the range of effort ratios quoted in the literature — from 30 to 120 per cent.

Thus it appears logical to relate the effort ratio to the predicted error level. This implies that the yardstick for the effort ratio should tend towards the lower part of the quoted range, below the 60 per cent level, for systems where the quality is expected to be very high; on the other hand, the effort ratio should be in the upper part of the range, above 60 per cent, for very complex systems where it will be difficult to achieve a high level of quality, and where the tests are very extensive. However, even if such weighting is used to reflect the quality level of the system, it is evident that any such ball-park prediction is still somewhat questionable.

Published yardsticks for the timescale of the tests are similar to those quoted for the test effort, but they are even less reliable because there are more uncertainties and variables; for example, the duration is much affected by the availability of programmers to solve the problems, and by the queuing and waiting times for corrections. The timescale also depends on any overlap of the coding and integration, and on any concurrent tests. It is therefore inadvisable to use yardstick ratios for the test timescale, other than for a very coarse prediction which should be made by an experienced person who can take account of the variables.

A.8.4 Advantages of the planned method

The uncertainties in the above yardsticks illustrate why it is advisable to examine the testing process in more depth — and this implies planning how the testing will actually be carried out. Some benefits of this approach are as follows:

- The schedule of test increments provides a practical and visible justification of the estimates.
- The schedule and estimate have a documented basis which can be examined and questioned; for example, the rate of error correction and the correcting effort, and these factors are measurable and controllable by management as described in Chapter 5.
- A considered judgement can be made of the residual errors because they are a proportion of those in the system test, and this helps to commit to an operational reliability target.

The method for estimating the resources and timescale will now be described separately for the integration and system test; although the details are presented in different ways for each test, the underlying approach is the same.

A.9 Integration testing

Building the system involves the progressive knitting together of the modules for entry to the system test. Each increment in the building process should test the correct construction of the joined modules — the software interfaces and those functions which spread over more than one of the modules. These tests are sometimes referred to as 'structural' tests because they are more concerned with the correct internal working of the system components — in contrast with the system tests which are more orientated to the response of the system to the external functions.

Although the building process can, and should, be predicted for each project, there is no standard model. Thus the plan has to be tailored to provide the required organisation of the test increments to match any overlap with coding and to provide the required depth of structural testing. The predicted depth of testing will substantially affect the estimate and, although more stringent testing in integration reduces the extent of the subsequent system test, it prolongs the integration process; therefore a balance has to be struck to optimise the combined effort and timescale of both tests.

A.9.1 Planning and estimating

The steps are similar to those for the programming stages.

Step A. The organisation of work

This is expressed as a schedule of increments, and the tasks and resources for each should be defined within a work package.

(Note. Any part of integration which is overlapped with coding also needs to be estimated since it will not be known whether the coding or the integration is the critical path of the project; for example, excessive use of programmers for error correction will dilute the coding effort and prolong that timescale and, on the other hand, any delay in the integrating process will reduce the overlap and extend the critical path of the integration testing.)

Step B. Estimating effort and timescale

In using the model described in Section A.8 it is assumed that there are two sequential phases of activity within each build increment. The first phase is for the 're-work' — the correction of the errors. The second phase is the forecast duration for the building and testing processes and verification of results.

Few published figures are available of errors arising in integration testing, probably because the extent of the task varies so much from project to project. However, Musa *et al.* (1987) give a considerable amount of historical data for errors arising in the system test; this indicates that an average of 4.5 errors per KLOC may be corrected, although the actual figures vary widely. As stated in the preceding section, it is likely that the errors generated in both tests will be between about three and ten per KLOC for most systems of reasonable quality. If it is speculatively assumed that an equal number of errors is corrected in each test, the errors emerging in integration testing would be within the range of $1-6$ per KLOC.

An example of the estimating method for integration testing is shown in Table A.3. This assumes that the errors are evenly distributed throughout the test increments, and that the average effort required for error correction is half a man-day per error; this compares with the assumption that one man-day is used for correcting one fault in system testing — because such faults are usually more difficult to deal with than those found in integration.

Table A.3 Estimating the integration tests

Increment	Idealised build timescale	Errors	Re-work effort
1	1 day	24	12 man-days
n	—	—	—
Total	5 days	120	60 man-days

The following additional assumptions are also made:

- the idealised timescale for each increment is one day,
- there are five sequential increments,
- there is a dedicated integration team of two staff,
- the prediction of total errors is 120.

Extending the table to show the re-work timescale depends on the corrective effort supplied by the programmers. Assuming that an average of 20 per cent of a team of twenty programmers is applied, then four man-days of effort is used each day to carry out the twelve man-days of corrective work for Increment 1. Thus, if there is no waiting time, the re-work will take three elapsed days and the total timescale for that increment is then the one day for the idealised test, plus the three days for the re-work. Similar estimates for the other four increments give a total timescale of twenty days for the complete test.

The summarised results are therefore:

Overall timescale = 20 days
Test effort = 20 × 2 (staff in test team) = 40 man-days
Re-work effort = 60 man-days from 20 staff

Step C. Producing the activity plan

This is the schedule of test increments, incorporating the timescale estimates and taking account of any overlapping.

Step D. Staff schedule

Whilst the planning, preparation and conduct of the test is carried out by the dedicated test team, the part-time use of programmers usually means that they are diverted from other activities. The extent of this diversion can be forecast, as shown in Table A.4, to indicate the impact on the other activities and to identify any 'spare' time. This illustrates how an increasing number of programmers become available for other work as the coding is completed.

Table A.4 Scheduling the use of programmers in integration

Week	1	2	4
Total programming staff	20	20	20
Average staff required for re-work	4	4	4
Average staff required for coding	12	10	8
Average no. of 'free' staff	4	6	8

The uncertainties in the process can be evaluated, as for the other stages, by setting minimum and maximum timescales and also by allowing for a contingency for the uncertain costs.

(More technical guidance on integration testing can be obtained from the specialised literature, such as the books by M. Deutsch and R. Wills 1988, B. Beiser 1983 and M.W. Evans 1984.)

A.10 System testing

This test, which commences after the final build and integration increment has been completed, aims to demonstrate that the total system works correctly and meets the requirements; the 'total' system means that the software should be tested with the operational hardware. The process is sometimes described as 'black box' testing since it is orientated to the external or user view of the system.

The test should be sufficiently stringent to give confidence that the system is fit for operational running; this intention may be demonstrated in planning any subsequent acceptance test before live running by assuming that such a test will demonstrate the fitness of the system without revealing new errors, except where the system test has been deliberately extended.

The following two main types of test are carried out:

• those relating to the functional requirements which check that the operational behaviour of the system is correct;

• those which test the technical performance and system behaviour under specified variations of the operational environment.

A.10.1 The planning outline

It is assumed that the test consists of a number of increments, or sub-tests, which progressively expose the system to the full requirement. An increment may also be defined as a work package, the completion of which represents a measurable achievement of a test milestone. The test increments are usually arranged so that the functional requirements are tested first, followed by the technical aspects, including the stress tests of performance and resilience.

Using the same simple model of the test as described in Section A.8, each test increment is composed of the following consecutive and limiting activities.

Phase 1 Correction of errors;
Phase 2 Verification tests.

Because the activities in Phase 1 occupy most of the total timescale, and are also more difficult to predict, attention is concentrated on how to estimate that portion of the test.

A.10.2 Forecasting the errors

In line with preceding predictions, and given a good standard of quality control, it is suggested that the target be set in the range between two and six errors per KLOC. This implies that error levels outside this range are exceptional and have the following implications:

- If the number of errors much exceeds the suggested higher level, the preceding development is of poor quality; and the need for such a large amount of error correction will not only escalate the test duration, but, because the residual errors are in proportion to those detected, it will result in an unreliable operational system.
- On the other hand, if the errors are much less than the suggested lower limit, the system test will have a relatively short timescale, followed by good operational reliability; such an optimistic scenario is more likely to apply to relatively small or simpler systems with a very high standard of quality control, but even here, it is more prudent to make a conservative forecast because a better achievement than planned will be welcome!

A.10.3   Forecasting the rate of progress for error correction

It is assumed that the test follows the pattern shown in Figure A.6, where the rate of error correction gradually declines during each increment. Although the time to correct each error will vary, depending on its difficulty and the skill of the corrector, the average rate of error correction for planning purposes is assumed as one per man-day (Musa *et al.*, 1987). Use of an average rate should be justified for a large project with many errors.

To ensure that progress in the tests is not held up by lack of computer time, there should be a contingency provision for additional shift working. As mentioned in Section A.3, the data given by Musa *et al.* (1987) may help to gauge the computer testing time during the correction limited phase; this suggests that an average amount of CPU computer time is required for the correction of a failure (this assumes the use of a computer with a given processing rate).

An example which illustrates how to calculate the approximate timescale for the error correction phase is given below:

Assume the following:

System size = 100 K instructions
Number of errors @ 4 per 1 K instruction = 400
Average error correction rate = 1 error per man-day
Total number of programming staff = 20
Average staff deployed on error correction each day = 5
Average errors corrected each day = 5 errors
Timescale for correcting 400 errors = 400/5 = 80 days

This example illustrates why it is necessary for the project manager to endorse the estimate; the above variables depend on judgements about how the project will be managed, including staff availability, skill levels and the degree of quality control.

A.10.4   *Producing the test schedule and estimate*

This follows the sequence of steps used for the preceding stages:

Step A.   *The outline test schedule*

A possible sequence of test increments is as follows:

(a)   functional tests performed in some graduated manner;
(b)   functional tests performed dynamically to replicate operational use;
(c)   all exception tests;
(d)   all stress testing and other tests to meet the technical requirements.

The work package(s) for each test increment should define the following:

• the tasks of the system team in conducting and controlling the tests, including verification of the corrections;
• the tasks involved in the correction phase, they should include a manual inspection before machine testing;
• the success criteria for the test increment, for example the maximum permitted number of unresolved errors;
• the budgeted provision of machine time.

Step B.   *Estimates of resource and timescale*

Estimates are made for the following three types of resource:

1.   Effort to conduct the tests. This comprises the system planning team and operators; the staffing is usually at a constant level throughout the test, although it may be boosted by secondment of some programmers if there is an overload.
2.   Correcting effort. This is estimated, as described in the preceding section.
3.   Computing time. In addition to the yardstick for the time for error correction a forecast has to be made of the time for the test runs; this has to be judged from the test schedule, with an allowance made for repeated tests. This resource may be critical in the test-limited phase where a shortage of machine time may delay progress unless compensated by shift working and staff overtime.

Using the same figures as in the preceding example for calculating the error correction phase, the overall timescale and staffing for the tests may be shown as in Table A.5.

In Table A.5 the timescale for each increment is obtained by adding the days for the corrective phase to those for the test phase. (The test phase was assumed to occupy 20 per cent of the total duration.) The system staffing for controlling the test is obtained by multiplying the number of staff by the total duration — of both phases of the test. But, one of the more difficult predictions is the number of programmers for the correcting work — this depends on the number of staff who can be made readily available from any other activities in which they are engaged.

Table A.5   Estimate of system testing

Increment	Corrective phase			Test phase		System effort man-days	Overall days
	Effort man-days	Av. staff	Days	Staff	Days		
1	40	5	8	4	2	40	10
⋮	⋮	⋮	⋮	⋮	⋮	⋮	⋮
10	40	5	8	4	2	40	10
Total	400	5	80	4	20	400	100

Step C. The activity plan

This is represented by the planned sequence of tests, taking account of any concurrency of test increments when aggregating their timescales.

Step D. Staffing schedule

Because only a proportion of the total programmer staffing is required for error correction, it is necessary to plan how the remaining effort can be used effectively.

A.10.5   Risk assessment

The uncertainties should be quantified by determining the earliest and latest completion dates, and the minimum and maximum costings. The longest timescale should make allowance for the following:

- a greater number of errors than predicted;
- a slower rate of error correction than forecast;
- shortage of machine time;
- unavailability of key staff.

Any of these variables will cause the schedule to slip; and this may be obvious by the need for an excessive number of repeated tests or by long waiting times for error correction. Bearing in mind that some difficult judgements have to be made in producing the estimate, it is likely that the forecasts of the earliest and latest schedules will differ by at least 25 per cent; however, it should be possible to keep within that range because of the in-built contingency of overtime and shift working. It is probable that there will be much more overtime during this stage than at other times in the project; and this should be reflected in the cost forecast.

A.11   System introduction and summary of system tasks

A.11.1   System introduction

The scope of this stage depends so much on the particular project that it is only possible to give a few general guidelines. On the assumption that there is a separate operational authority, distinct from the project, the main project tasks are usually as follows:

- installing the hardware and software products;
- assisting the operational management to plan the initial use of the system;
- developing and installing the initial data records;
- loading the system and providing close support to the operational staff in resolving problems;
- correcting defects;
- carrying out any residual acceptance tests.

The forecast of the project effort and timescale depends on the particular loading plan for the system and on the outstanding tasks required to meet the acceptance criteria. A planned amount of effort must be provided, albeit by part-time programmers, to correct the initial teething problems until the level of service is acceptable, and their composite skills must cover all parts of the system. Some full-time project staff are also required to provide the first-line problem solving capability, to orchestrate the final testing and installation of changes to the hardware and software, and also to guide and develop the operational and maintenance staff.

A.11.2 Summary of system resources

In addition to the staff scheduled for the integration and system tests and the system introduction, system staff are also required for the following tasks:

- modifying the design proposal and user requirements, including resolution of queries from both programming and user staff;
- detailed design and planning of the integration and system testing, including inspection of the test specifications;
- operation of the computer test system;
- other related development tasks, one of the most important of which is for the preparation of the initial data records which involve both system and programmer staff and which may be regarded as a separate mini-project.

These resources can usually be gauged fairly easily. Apart from the test operators, the system team is of fairly constant size throughout the project timescale, and it is only a small proportion of the overall staffing.

A.12 Management, ancillary and support tasks

This resource may amount to between one-quarter and one-half of the total staff, depending on the nature of the project. An indication of the particular tasks which most vary in scope is given below. Any constructional tasks, such as the production of project standards, should be prescribed and scheduled by activity plans, and these plans should synchronise with those for the main productive activities so that the supporting aids are available in good time.

A check list of tasks is given below (these items are also included within the overall outline of the Work Breakdown Structure given at the end of Chapter 4):

1. Management, including the direction and supervision of all other project staff.
2. *Manual production, i.e. reference specifications and manuals which describe the developed system and the manuals for using, operating and maintaining the system.
3. *Training, i.e. for project staff and for the users to operate and maintain the system.
4. Quality control, i.e. for producing the project standards and for monitoring their application in all project activities.
5. *Procurement and installation of all hardware and other ancillary products.
6. *Installation and maintenance of the development test system.
7. *Recruitment and training of new project staff.
8. Accounting functions.
9. Clerical and typing tasks.
10. Other administrative tasks relating to the accommodation and general office services required for the project team, for example catering, cleaning, telephones, security.

The tasks marked with an asterisk vary considerably, depending on the particular project and on variables such as the following:

*   the extent and novelty of the hardware;
*   whether contractor or internal staffing is used;
*   the extent of the publications;
*   the required amount of training;
*   the extent and distribution of the system and the user population;
*   the need to recruit many staff and to hire staff from contractors;
*   the use of novel project tools.

A.13 Summary

The overall staffing can be presented within schedules which show the numbers on a week-to-week basis. Similarly, an outline activity plan should be produced to demonstrate both optimistic and conservative timescales. The staff schedules may be summarised as shown in Figure A.8, which should be useful in communicating with the directing management who approve the estimates; and the summary indicates how both staff numbers and cost vary in each of the two estimating scenarios.

Figure A.8 Summary
of staffing estimate

Staff task	Staff number Week 1 ... Week n	Effort (man-weeks)	Extra effort for late completion
Programmers • design • coding • tests • introduction			
System staff • tests • introduction • other			
Ancillaries			
Support staff			
Management			
Total no.			
Staff cost contingency			
Maximum cost			

Earliest
completion

Latest
completion

The plans and estimates should also be presented at lower levels:

• Firstly, the cost should be calculated for each heading on the Work Breakdown
  Structure to allow a more detailed examination of any particular type of project
  expense; the total cost of all work packages should also match that shown
  in the staffing summary in Figure A.8, and this should be a useful reconciliation
  check that the work packages are comprehensive and match the activity plans.
• Secondly, the detailed activity plan and staff schedules, as indicated in Figure
  A.3, should provide the supporting detail for examining the timescale and cost
  of all development activities.

References

Albrecht, A.J. and Gaffney, J.E., Jr 'Software function, source lines of code and development effort prediction — a software science validation', *IEEE Transactions on Software Engineering*, **SE-9**, (6), pp. 639–47, 1983.

Beiser, B. *Software Testing Techniques*, Van Nostrand Reinhold, 1983.

Boehm, B.W. *Software Engineering Economics*, Prentice Hall, 1981.

Boehm, B.W. 'Software engineering economics', *IEEE Transactions on Software Engineering*, **SE10**, Jan. 1984.

Boehm, B.W. 'Improving software productivity', *Computer*, pp. 43–57, Sept. 1987.

Deutsch, M.S. and Wills, R.R. *Software Quality Engineering*, Prentice Hall, 1988.

Dyer, M. 'Designing software for provable correctness', in *A Software Life Cycle*, Ince, D. and Andrews, D. (eds.), Butterworths, 1990.

Evans, M.W. *Productive Software Test Management*, John Wiley, 1984.

Fagan, M.E. 'Design and code inspections to reduce errors in program development'. *IBM System Journal*, **15** (3), pp. 182–211, 1976.

Fagan, M.E. 'Advances in software inspections', *IEEE Transactions on Software Engineering*, pp. 79–87, July 1986.

Grady, R.B. and Caswell, D.L. *Software Metrics: Establishing a company-wide program*, Prentice Hall, 1987.

IEE Publication, *Software Inspection Handbook*, 1990.

IEE Publication, *Software Quality Assurance: Model procedures*, 1990.

IEE Publication, *Guidelines for the Documentation of Computer Software for Real-time and Interactive Systems* (2nd edn), 1990.

Jones, C. *Programming Productivity*, McGraw-Hill, 1986.

Kemerer, C. 'An empirical validation of software cost estimating models', *Communications of the ACM*, **30**, (5), pp. 416–29, 1987.

Kitchenham, B.A. and Taylor, N.R. 'Software cost models', *ICL Technical Journal*, May 1984.

Kitchenham, B.A., Kitchenham, A.P. and Fellows, J.P, 'The effects of inspections on software quality and productivity', *ICL Technical Journal*, May 1986.

Kitchenham, B.A. 'Management metrics', in *Software Reliability: Achievement and assessment*, B. Littlewood (ed.), Blackwell Scientific, 1987.

Londeix, B. *Cost Estimation for Software Development*, Addison-Wesley, 1987.

Macro, A. and Buxton, J. *The Craft of Software Engineering*, Addison-Wesley, 1987.

Musa, J.D., Iannino, A. and Okumuto, K. *Software Reliability — Measurement, Prediction, Application*. McGraw-Hill, 1987.

Putnam, L.H. : Tutorial, Software Cost Estimating and Life-cycle Control, IEEE Computer Society, COMPSAC 80, IEEE Catalog No. EHO 165-1, NY Oct. 1980.

Sommerville, I. (ed.), *Software Engineering Environments*, Peter Peregrinus 1986.

STARTS Purchasers' Handbook, NCC Publications 1988.

STARTS Developers' Guide, NCC Publications 1988.

Takahashi, M. and Kamayachi, Y. 'An empirical study of the model for program error prediction', *The Proceedings of the 8th International Conference on Software Engineering*, London, pp. 330–36, August 1985.

US Department of Defense Draft Standard, *Defense System Software Development*, DOD-STD-2167A, 15 August 1986.

Index